CW01507543

Northern Ireland on a Plate

Food by Northern Ireland's finest chefs
and restaurants.
Edited by **Ferrier Richardson**

Introduction

Welcome to Northern Ireland on a Plate. Firstly can I thank my great friend Noel McMeel – award winning chef, worldwide Culinary Ambassador for Northern Ireland, and all-round good guy for helping me put together this great line up of venues and chefs within the book. Also for introducing me to his wonderful friends Geraldine Hughes and Conor Allen who have contributed the forward for the book. Without your local knowledge and advice this book would not be the book that it is, I am eternally grateful to you and hope you are proud of what the "On a Plate Team" have delivered.

It is interesting to see how the way we now perceive restaurants and how we use them has changed over the years. I believe we still look for excellence and value for money whatever level we are dining at, but at the same time we now look for a more relaxed environment, professional friendly service and hospitality as opposed to dining in a pretentious venue who think they are better than their customers, stiff service or having to pay homage to a plate of food or God forbid a chef with an ego.

I believe all the restaurants featured within the book are providing these positive qualities within their venues, whether they have a Michelin Star, Bib Gourmand, Good Food Guide recognition or not.

The number one common denominator in all these great venues as well as giving us a big warm Northern Irish hug is their commitment to excellence and their dedication to make sure the people who are supporting them get the best experience possible every time they walk over the door and into "their home".

The last few years have not been great for the hospitality sector, but through it all these wonderful operations and operators have proven they are survivors and are prepared to deliver a first class product and experience no matter what the economic climate is throwing at them, always making a point of utilising Northern Ireland's great larder, supporting local artisan suppliers and at the same time maximising sustainability and seasonality wherever possible.

Each venue has a unique story to tell within their chapter in the book, they all share an insight into their daily routines, unique selling points, their restaurant's philosophy and a bit of "Craic" thrown in along the way, thanks to Alex Meikle's charm and ingenuity when interviewing them.

I would like to think that the way the book has been put together by all the team and contributors will encourage you to try these wonderful recipes at home, or even better still, will make you want to visit these beautiful and wonderful venues, support them and enjoy their unique interiors, wonderful hospitality and great food.

Can I ask that you always remember to thank your server and kitchen team if you have had a great experience and to put a nice post up on the likes of Trip Advisor or Google, these kind gestures mean a lot to us all in the industry and encourage us to keep coming back every day and adding another layer of varnish to enhance our quality product.

Thank you for supporting the book, but even more can I thank you for supporting all our contributors within Northern Ireland and the Irish hospitality industry, as I believe without all the commitment and dedication these venues and operators provide on a daily basis, our lives would be a lot poorer without them.

Many thanks,

Ferrier Richardson
Owner and editor of the On a Plate book series

First published in 2025

FR On A Plate

Glasgow, Scotland

ISBN 978-1-0682060-1-6

Photography

Meagan Daley Studio

Design

River Runs Deep

Copywriting

Alex Meikle

Administration

Vicki Robertson

Editor

Ferrier Richardson

Print

J Thomson Colour Printers. Glasgow

www.carbonbalancedprint.com
CBP2296

Foreword

Northern Ireland is a place reborn – vibrant, spirited, and bursting with talent.

Its energy infuses every part of life, and in this book, we're thrilled to explore one of its most exciting expressions: the culinary scene. Here, we spotlight just a few of the remarkable talents that call this island home.

The dark days of the past – the Troubles, the fear, the division – are behind us. In their place, a new spirit of celebration and unity has emerged. And what better way to honour that than by breaking bread together? We've travelled the world and tasted its most indulgent cuisines, but nothing compares to returning home to Ireland and savouring the flavours born of its green fields and rich soil.

There's something deeply intimate about sharing food with those you love. It's one of life's most meaningful acts. Northern Ireland, once scarred by conflict, has not only survived – it has flourished. Out of the ashes has risen a culinary movement led by passionate chefs, bakers, and makers. Their dedication and creativity are palpable in every dish, every bite, every bold flavour.

One of the greatest joys of coming home – besides hugging our loved ones – is eating! Oysters from Carlingford Lough, fresh fish from the northern coast, golden creamy butter, and lush, decadent desserts. Need we say more?

Fifteen years ago, we believed a couple of barmen from the Merchant Hotel belonged on the world stage in cities like New York or London. That belief sparked the long journey that became The Dead Rabbit. Today, it no longer feels necessary for Northern Ireland's culinary talent to leave – because the world is coming here. Northern Ireland is becoming a stage of its own, attracting the curious and rewarding the adventurous.

This book is a celebration of what can flourish when a place emerges from darkness into light. It's a far cry from the brown sauce sandwiches of old – and a delicious glimpse into the future.

As you taste your way through these pages, meeting the people and stories behind each dish, you will be reminded time and again of what makes this place so special. The food here isn't just about ingredients – it's about heritage, resilience, creativity, and heart. And the best part? This is just the beginning. Here's to many more meals, more discoveries, and more moments shared around the table. We hope this book inspires you to taste, to explore, and to celebrate the incredible food and spirit of Northern Ireland.

Geraldine & Conor

Geraldine Hughes & Conor Allen

Geraldine Hughes Award winning actress, writer, director, and producer and a patron of the Integrated Education Fund.

Conor Allen Serial entrepreneur in the United States. Conor, amongst his many successful ventures, was instrumental in creating The Dead Rabbit in New York that has now spawned multiple venues across the U.S. The Dead Rabbit has been voted the best bar in the world, amongst their many international accolades.

Acknowledgements

Northern Ireland on a Plate is long overdue, due to the enormous changing face of its wonderful culinary scene within this beautiful country and the excellent chefs operating within it today.

To showcase these wonderful restaurants and their chefs you need an exceptional team of a great designer, writer, inspirational photographer and a meticulous administrator to make it all happen.

I believe one of my strengths is that I can put together award winning teams, be that for an international culinary Olympic event, a charity event to raise money for a great cause, a high-class restaurant, a five-star hotel opening or for a Head of State.

Northern Ireland on a Plate would not have been possible without the creative flair and organisational expertise of the following.

Stuart Gilmour, from River Runs Deep, Glasgow, who has now designed this book, Edinburgh and the best-selling Glasgow on a Plate 3 book from top to toe and has way exceeded my expectations on all these projects. Anyone who has any design projects in the pipeline, Stuart would be your go to guy. He is truly exceptional and anyone who knows me well will know I do not dish out praise like this without it being earned.

Meagan Daley for all her wonderful photography and dedication to the project. It has been a joy working with you Meagan, your enthusiasm and dedication has been a constant throughout the project and I look forward to working with you on future On a Plate books.

The amazing and wonderful wordsmith Alex Meikle who has brought the chef's words to life and dance on the first page of each chapter, once again it has been a joy Alex, your dry humour has kept us all going throughout the project.

Our administrator and head girl Vicki Robertson, who has been responsible for bringing the project together. An arduous task for anyone, given the difficulty of getting hold of our chefs, getting them to respond to deadlines and ensuring all the recipes all made sense. Thank you for your tenacity, professionalism and energy throughout this journey.

The wonderful Noel McMeel for his local knowledge and perseverance in helping me get the Chefs and Restaurants on board. Also for introducing me to Conor and Geraldine who did the beautiful and inspirational forward to the book. The book would have not been the same without you all.

To all the talented award-winning chefs who have contributed to the book, without your culinary prowess this project would not have been the same and I hope you all feel the On a Plate team have done your talents justice, showcasing your beautiful dishes.

The star who is Angela McCrae at Waterstones who believed in the On a Plate project from the get-go and gave me great advice all along our journey and all the wonderful staff who work in Waterstones fabulous stores and promote the books with such enthusiasm and professionalism. Thank you all from the bottom of my heart.

Lastly to you the reader, without your support this book would not exist and for that I and everyone involved with the project are forever grateful. I hope that each chapter will encourage and inspire you to visit and support all the wonderful restaurants within this book.

Many thanks,

Ferrier Richardson
Owner and editor of the On a Plate book series

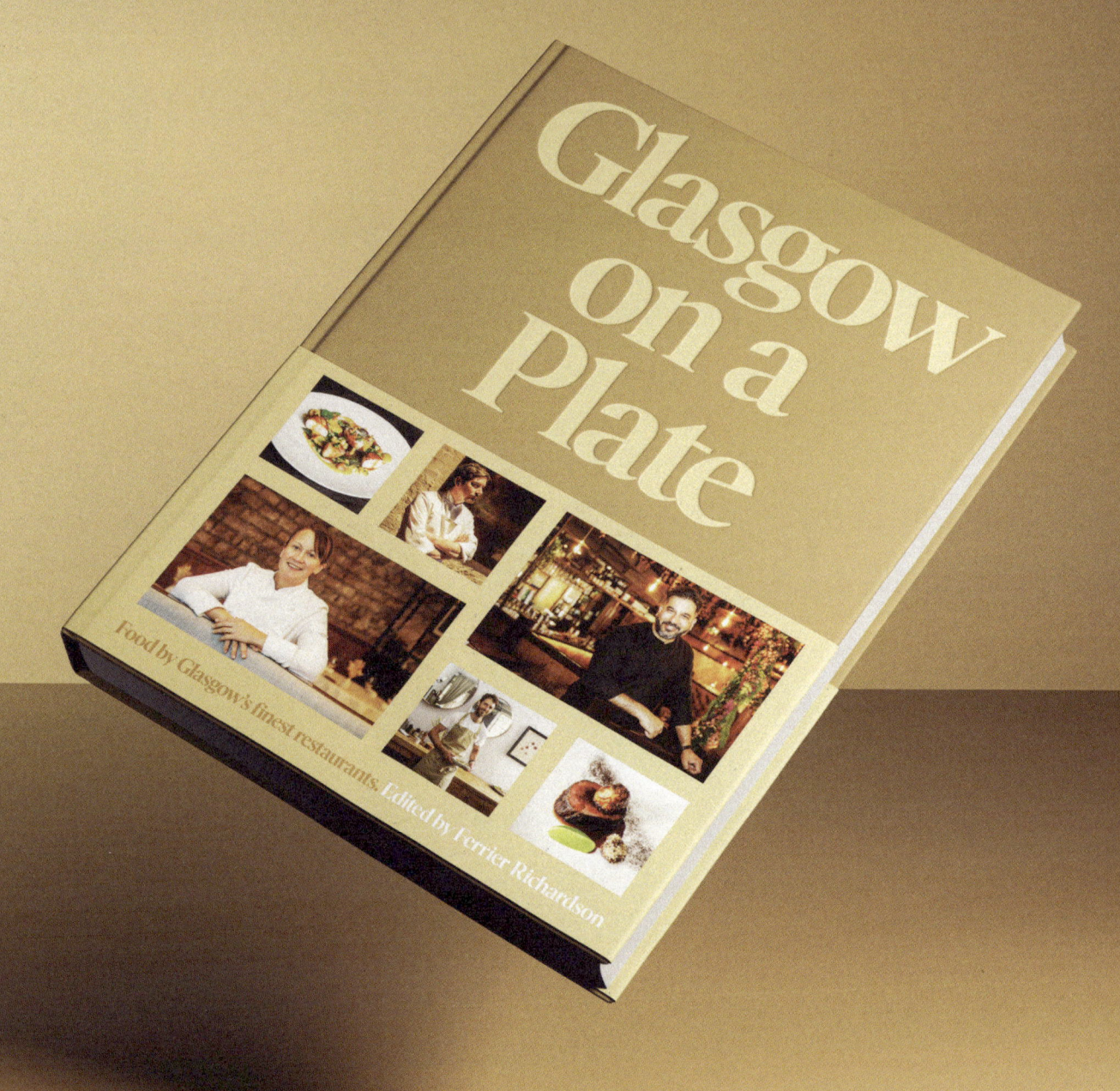

Glasgow on a Plate.

Available from waterstones.com

While stocks last.

Edinburgh on a Plate.
Available from waterstones.com

Contents

01

The Old Inn
Andy Turner
Executive chef

"My philosophy of food is, keep it simple, use what's locally available and in season around you."

The Old Inn is a charming Victorian era coach inn located on the Co. Down coast of Northern Ireland. It has become renowned as a foodie destination receiving 1 AA Rosette status in 2020 and is the perfect backdrop for deluxe brasserie dining where seasonal Irish produce is always on the menu.

I've always loved cooking (my grandmother was a chef) and I figured with choosing dining as a career, I'd always be in a job as everybody must eat! While at college I was fortunate to receive great training from three Italian brothers who were all chefs and who had worked under Anton Mosimann at the Dorchester Hotel. At 19, they sent me to work with Chef Clive Howell at the Lygon Arms Hotel in the Cotswolds where I received a good grounding. Next, I worked with a host of fantastic chefs including Paul Gayler and Marco Pierre White. I spent time in some great kitchens overseas, beginning in Sydney where I was Head Chef at the Bennelong at the Opera House before opening my own restaurant which received a Sydney Morning Herald "Chef's Hat". This was followed by stints in the Caribbean and Japan before settling in Ireland.

I worked for ten years in Dublin, mainly with Oliver Dunne from Bon Appetit and Ross Lewis from Chapter One before coming to Northern Ireland with my wife to set up our own restaurant 'Hara'. It was recommended in the Michelin Guide. During lockdown we turned our hand to producing gourmet food boxes for pickup - named Hara at Home, which is still very much in business.

I started at the Old Inn, Crawfordsburn in 2023 and I'm now Executive Head Chef. Highlights on the menu include duck egg mayonnaise with shaved duck and chateaubriand of Irish beef,

while more casual fare is served at the 1614 Bar including Walter Ewings smoked salmon and chicken and leek pie. We also serve a popular and delicious afternoon tea.

Northern Ireland has some fantastic game, meat and cheeses and we focus on local produce that includes locally supplied potatoes, asparagus grown under glass, seaweeds and brilliant shellfish.

My philosophy of food is, keep it simple, use what's locally available and in season around you. We always have classics on the menu such as steak and fish and chips.

We're always busy; on a Sunday we can serve up to 450 people. Our impressive private dining rooms can host banquets for 20 to 45 guests. There is a brigade of fifteen in the kitchen to make all this happen.

The Old Inn appeals to all ages as overnight guests can avail themselves of the Treetop Spa, while local people can enjoy the 1614 Bar for drinks and snacks and there's always a friendly welcome for four legged friends walking in the neighbouring Crawfordsburn Country Park.

The hotel is situated in a superb location in Northern Ireland just fifteen minutes outside Belfast at the edge of Crawfordburn Country Park on an old coaching route.

Northern Ireland has some excellent restaurants and a thriving dining scene, and I'm thrilled that Old Inn is an important and iconic part of that.

Duck egg mayonnaise, fried bread, smoked duck

Ingredients

Dressing

Chardonnay vinegar - 100ml
Pomace oil - 200ml
Cloves garlic - 2
Shallot - 1
Tarragon - 2 sprigs
Salt and pepper

Mayonnaise

Egg yolks - 4
White wine vinegar - 50ml
Dijon mustard - 50ml
Neutral rapeseed oil - 250ml
Salt
Smoked paprika
Cayenne pepper

Acidic Onions

Spanish onions - 2 large
White wine vinegar - 100ml
White wine - 100ml
Dijon mustard - 25ml
Horseradish cream - 25ml
Crème Fraiche - 100ml

Fried bread

Brioche loaf
Duck fat

Apple balsamic gel

Apple balsamic - 250ml
Sugar - 60g
Ultratex - 30g

For the plate

Duck eggs - 4
Red onions - 2 medium
Acidic onions
Mayonnaise
Dressing
Fried brioche
Smoked duck
Celery salt
Herbs and pea shoot to garnish

Method

Serves 4

Here's a take on a classic starter that we all enjoyed back in the day. Hope you enjoy.

For the dressing Mix all together and allow to sit for 24 hrs before use.

For the mayonnaise Whisk the yolks, vinegar, mustard together. Drizzle in the oil and emulsify. Season to taste.

For the acidic onions Finely dice the onions. Cover with the white wine and the vinegar, and reduce until the pan is dry. Cool.

When the onions are cold, mix in the mustard, horseradish and crème fraîche. Season.

For the fried bread Break the brioche into small pieces and fry in duck fat until golden.

For the apple balsamic gel Whisk all together and allow the Ultratex to thicken the vinegar.

For the plate Bring a medium sized pan of water up to the boil. Meanwhile peal and cut your onions in half – length ways.

When your water is boiling gently drop in the duck eggs and onions and simmer for 7 and a half mins. When cooked refresh the eggs in iced water to stop them cooking any further. Remove the onion and allow to drain but do not cool. Season with the celery salt and dress while still hot, with the dressing.

Peal your duck eggs, and cut in half – the yolk should still be soft. Season with the celery salt.

Dress the plate Spoon a little of the acidic onion in the bottom of the bowl. Arrange the eggs and red onions on top. Add a few dots of mayonnaise and apple balsamic vinegar. Then arrange the sliced smoked duck and crispy fried bread around the plate and finish with the herbs and pea shoots.

< Duck egg mayonnaise, fried bread, smoked duck

Page 20 Kilkeel crab, Comber Earlies, asparagus and sea herbs

Black mountain lamb, Kearny blue, tapioca, peas and beans, black garlic

Ingredients

Pea purée

Butter - 25g

Onion - 100g

Garlic - 1 glove

Peas - 250g

Chicken stock - 100ml

Tapioca

Broad beans - 100g

Peas - 100g

Chicken stock - 1l

Water - 1l

Kearey blue cheese - 95g

Tapioca - 160g

Sour cream - 225g

Black mountain lamb

Lamb neck fillet - 1kg

Carrot - 1

Onion - 1

Celery - 1 stick

Leek

Thyme - 20g

Rosemary - 20g

Bay leaves - 2

Chicken stock - 1l

Lamb stock - 1l

For the plate

Black garlic - 1 bulb

Pea pods

Pea tendrils

Method

Serves 4

This is a dish we came up with when I was head chef at Chapter One – it's great comfort food.

The lamb Trim and sear the lamb. Place in oven tray and add the diced onion, carrot, celery, leek and the herbs, and cover with the stocks. Cover and cook in the oven at 145°C for 4/5 hrs, or until soft.

When cooked remove the lamb from the cooking liquor and pass. Reduce the stock until you have a glaze. Then roll your lamb in it, and keep hot – ready to serve.

The pea purée Sweat the onion and garlic in the butter. Add the peas. Cover with the chicken stock and cook for 2 mins. Blend and pass.

The Tapioca Blanch the beans and peas in boiling water. Remove and refresh. Add the chicken stock to the water and bring up to the boil. Rain in the tapioca and cook for 12 – 15 mins until soft. Drain and pass through a sieve. Put back into a pan and mix in the cheese and cream. Finish with the peas and beans.

To serve Spoon the pea purée on to a plate. Then spoon the tapioca. Place the glazed lamb in the middle. Arrange the black garlic, pea shoots and pods around the lamb.

< Black mountain lamb, Kearny blue, tapioca, peas and beans, black garlic

Page 21 Ginger custard, poached rhubarb with lemon and thyme

Kilkeel crab, Comber Earlies, asparagus and sea herbs

Ingredients

Cock brown crab - 1 large. Approx. 1kg
Comber Earlies - 600g
Northen Irish asparagus - 12 spears
Rape seed oil - 50g
Lemon juice - Juice of 1/2 lemon
Sea purslane - 30g
Sea beet - 12 leaves
Samphire - 40g
Lemon balm - 20g
Dilisk - 30g

The dressing

Chardonnay vinegar - 100ml
Pomace oil - 200ml
Garlic - 2 cloves
Shallot - 1
Tarragon - 2 sprigs
Salt and pepper

The crab mayonnaise

Egg yolks - 4
White wine vinegar - 50ml
Dijon mustard - 50ml
Brown crab meat from the crab - 100g
Neutral rapeseed oil - 250ml
Salt
Smoked paprika
Cayenne pepper

Method

Serves 4

If there's one dish that brings all of Northern Ireland together this has to be up there.

The dressing Mix all together and allow to sit for 24 hrs before use.

The crab mayonnaise Whisk the yolks, vinegar, mustard and brown crab meat together. Drizzle in the oil and emulsify. Season to taste.

The method Bring a large pot of water to the boil and season with salt – you need quite a lot of salt – it needs to taste of the sea. When the water is boiling drop in the crab, and cook for 12 – 15 mins. Drain and allow to cool.

Wash your potatoes and clean the skins, but don't peel. Cool until soft in boiling water. When cooked, drain and cool slightly. Slice and drizzle with the dressing and drop in the dilisk.

Peel and cook the asparagus. Refresh, wash and clean all of the sea herbs for your plate.

Now to prepare the cooked crab Remove all of the legs, and with short sharp taps with a clean hammer – crack the shell. Remove the white meat. Turn the body of the crab over push up the main body and the shell will pop off. Drain any water and scrape the shell to remove the brown meat for the mayonnaise. Give the main body a wash. Remove the dead man's fingers (the gills), and pick the remaining white meat. When you have removed all the crab, season and dress with the rapeseed oil and lemon juice.

Now just dress your plate with still warm potatoes. Cover with the dressed white crab, a few spoons of the brown crab mayonnaise. Cover with the sea herbs, asparagus and dilisk.

Ginger custard, poached rhubarb with lemon and thyme

Ingredients

Ginger custard

Gelatine - 4g leaf

Milk - 120ml

Egg yolk - 125g

Castor sugar - 25g

Golden syrup - 80g

Fresh ginger - 25g

Double cream - 375g

Gingerbread

Milk - 75g

Dark brown sugar - 60g

Butter - 60g

Golden syrup - 60g

Black treacle - 60g

Plain flour

Ground ginger - 20g

Soda - 3g

Egg - 1 small

Rhubarb and poaching syrup

Forced rhubarb - 750g

Sugar - 500g

Water - 500ml

Lemon - 1

Thyme - 20g

Rhubarb ice

Rhubarb poaching liquor - 500ml

Water - 450ml

To serve

Stem ginger - 25g

Sour cream - 80g

Lemon balm

Method

Serves 4

Who doesn't like Rhubarb and custard? This is a great dessert that can all be made the day before.

For the custard Bloom your gelatine in cold water. Slice the ginger and add to the milk, sugar, syrup in a sauce pan and simmer until all the sugars are dissolved.

Drop the soft gelatine into the milk, and pass through a sieve, now add your double cream and stir.

Pour into 4 even sized moulds and bake at 105°C for 35 mins until just set. Allow to cool for 1 hr and then freeze until hard, and remove from moulds, these can be stored in the freezer for up to a month.

For the gingerbread Pre-heat the oven to 160°C. In a saucepan heat the milk, butter, sugar syrup and treacle together until warm. Whisk in the flour, ginger and soda, and beat until cool. Finally, mix in the egg. Pour into a loaf tin and cook for 45 mins. Take out of the tin and allow to cool.

Slice a few fine slices, and break the rest into small pieces. Dry both in the oven at 60°C overnight. Blend the pieces into crumbs and keep in a air tight container.

Poached rhubarb Cut the rhubarb into batons. Bring the sugar, water, zest and juice of the lemon up to the boil and pour over the rhubarb. Cover and cook in the oven at 110°C for about 30 mins or until your rhubarb is soft. Cool overnight in the liquor.

Rhubarb ice Mix the cooking liquor and the water altogether and freeze.

To plate Take the frozen custard and coat in the gingerbread crumbs. Allow to defrost for 1 hr before serving. Place on top, a bundle of the rhubarb, a couple of slices stem ginger, a tbsp of sour cream, a scraping of rhubarb ice, and a few lemon balm leaves.

02

Gillies Grill
Callum Irwin
Senior sous chef

Gillies Grill is the headline restaurant within the Galgorm resort, which boasts four restaurants and a world-famous spa. It's a contemporary Irish restaurant that fuses with a dynamic range of Asian, Mediterranean and North African influences.

I started out in hospitality at 14, mainly to finance my golf hobby and could barely see over the large kitchen sink I was assigned to. I rapidly adapted and enjoyed the environment, the buzz, the passion and the smells of a kitchen. Early in my career I worked under a classically Michelin trained chef who I learned so much from, providing me with an understanding of textures, flavours, plating and butchery. That sparked my passion for cooking.

I went on to study Culinary Arts Management at the University of Ulster during weekdays while working in the prestigious The Muddlers Club in Belfast at weekends. I was part of the team who gained a Michelin star for the restaurant which it still holds. This was the period when I developed both my academic and professional career, achieving a first-class degree, winning Northern Ireland Masterchef in 2019, and a scholarship to Hong Kong in 2020.

I moved next to Edo, a Spanish tapas restaurant, then onto the Academy Training restaurant affiliated to Ulster University where I was Sous chef. I then became sous chef at Shu in Belfast, a large modern French restaurant. In the space of six years, I received a fantastic academic education and professional experience of many different cuisines, capacities and styles of restaurants.

More recently, I'm now senior sous chef with Gillies Grill at Galgorm. The restaurant is the hub of the hotel and serves excellent, largely locally produced, contemporary Northern Irish gastronomy.

Northern Ireland has an exceptional larder. Among highlights at Galgorm are east coast scallops, Glenarm short horn beef, Conway farm asparagus, Jawbox gin and Curly Pig's cured meats, all a part of the dishes I have created for this book.

Our customer base is diverse ranging from families to couples, weddings and other special occasions. Our ethos is that the guests' needs are our priority. We continually strive to exceed their expectations by providing them with exquisite food, excellent, warm service and a relaxing ambiance.

I'm delighted at the quality of the food we're producing combined with the cohesion of the team and the style of the service. It's commendable and a large part of that is down to the work of Dave Gilmore and Aaron Finlay the two executive chefs across the Galgorm complex. Northern Ireland has a fantastic hospitality scene with the Galgorm collection making an important contribution to that scene. I'm really proud to say I'm Northern Irish to showcase the quality of the ingredients and produce we have. We're now a destination for people from all cultures to visit and work in, typified by Galgorm which has people from all over the world working here. I'm delighted that Gillies Grill is part of that.

"The restaurant serves excellent, largely locally produced, contemporary Northern Irish gastronomy."

Conway Farm asparagus, chipotle hummus, puffed chickpea, bresaola, truffle egg yolk

Ingredients

Asparagus - 16 stalks. 4 per serving

Sorbet stock

Water - 375ml

Glucose - 375g

Chipotle hummus

Tinned chickpeas - 400g. Drained and rinsed

Rose harissa paste - 160g

Lemon juice - 45ml

Tahini - 100g

Extra virgin olive oil - 60ml

Season to taste

Puffed chickpeas

Chickpeas - 50g. Drained

Sumac - 1 tsp

Bresaola

Bresaola - Raw. Finely shaved.

Truffled yolk

Eggs - 6

Truffle oil - 20ml

Method

Serves 4

The asparagus Stalks removed – turned last inch. Cooked in a butter for approximately 90 secs. Charred on grill before serving.

The hummus Weigh all ingredients. Purée all together in robo coupe or food processor until a smooth solution has formed. Season with salt and white pepper to taste.

For the chickpeas Drain the chickpeas. Fry at 180°C until golden and crisp. Season with sumac and salt.

Bresaola Use a company called "curly pig" meats, a local Northern Irish based company who specialise in cured meats. The bresaola should be raw and finely shaved.

For the truffled yolk Cook whole egg at 56°C in shell. Then place into an ice bath. Remove from shell and remove egg white. Place the egg yolk into a mixing bowl and emulsify with truffle oil. Use straight away.

To serve Place the hummus on the base of the plate and level out with a spoon to create an even circle. Place the blanched/charred asparagus on this base evenly, dot the truffled egg yolk around the dish – roughly 6 – 7 dots is sufficient. Add three shavings of the bresaola and sprinkle the puffed chickpeas evenly across the asparagus and finish with fresh herbs.

< Conway Farm asparagus, chipotle hummus, puffed chickpea, bresaola, truffle egg yolk

Page 28 Scallop, chicken, pickled walnut ketchup, cauliflower, tarragon

Beef fillet, shortrib, broccoli purée, horseradish emulsion, blue cheese crumb, bone marrow jus

Ingredients

Fillets

Fillets - 4 x 250g approx portions. Trimmed and Portioned. A good beef fillet is key. I have used glenarm shorthorn beef, which has been hung for 30 days to improve the flavour and moisture content.

Braised short rib

Beef short rib - 1kg

Carrot - 1

Onion - 1

Celery - 2 sticks

Leek - 1/2

Garlic - 1 bulb

Rosemary - 5

Thyme - 5

Red wine - 1l

Beef stock - 1l

Water - 3l

Plating

Cooked short rib (above)

Shallot - 1

Dill - 10g. Picked

Dijon mustard - 1/2 tbsp

Broccoli purée

Broccoli - 1 head

Spinach - 100g

Vegetable stock - 200ml

Horseradish emulsion

Eggs - 2 yolks

Fresh grated horseradish - 1 tbsp

White wine vinegar - 1 tsp

Dijon mustard - 1 tsp

Vegetable oil - 300ml

Salt and white pepper

Young Buck blue crumb

Blue cheese - 100g

Panko breadcrumbs - 100g

Parsley - 25g chopped

Dill - 25g chopped

Garlic powder - 1/2 tsp

Olive oil - 2 tbsp

Bonemarrow jus

Reduced liquor off short rib

Bone marrow bone - 1

Method

Braised short rib Prepare all vegetables. Remove excess fat from the short rib and cut into two bone sections. Preheat the oven at 160°C. Seal both sides of the short rib in a saucepan over a high heat with vegetable oil. Place into a deep oven dish. Using the same pan, colour the prepped vegetables. Pour wine over the veg and reduce by half. Place into an oven dish with th short rib. Pour over water and stock. Ensure the beef and vegetables are fully submerged. Double cover the oven dish with tinfoil shiny side down. Place into the oven for 4 hrs at 160°C.

Plating the short rib Once finished, remove the bone from the rib, and pick down, removing all excess fat. Pass the liquid left in the oven dish into a large saucepan and reduce until a viscous jus like liquid is achieved. Use this liquid to bind the short rib before serving. Add diced shallot, chopped dill and Dijon mustard to the beef. Season with coarse salt and black pepper. Place into an onion cup, and run through the oven.

Broccoli purée Place a large saucepan of water and salt onto a high heat and allow to boil. Prepare the broccoli into even sized florets. Use waste for a stock. Place the broccoli into boiling salty water for 7 mins. Add to a stand blender with the spinach and vegetable stock and blitz thoroughly. Pass through a fine sieve and cool over ice.

Horseradish emulsion Place all ingredients apart from oil into a suitable container. Using a stick blender, slowly pour the oil over the other ingredients while blending.

Young buck blue crumb Combine all ingredients in a mixing bowl. Place into a preheated oven at 180°C for 10 mins. Mix and bake for another 10 mins (or until a golden brown colour has been achieved).

Bonemarrow jus Bake the bone in a preheated oven at 180°C. Remove interior marrow using a butter knife, boil pre reduced stock from the short rib and emulsify the marrow into the sauce using a hand blender.

To serve Finish the onion cup with the braised short rib with blue cheese crumb, and place on the top right hand side of the plate. Spoon the broccoli purée onto the bottom right hand side of the plate. Place a large dot of the horseradish emulsion on the top left of the plate and cover with chopped chives. Slice the rested fillet in half lengthways and season with rock salt and place on the bottom left of the plate. Spoon over the bone marrow jus across the top of the beef fillet and serve.

< Beef fillet, shortrib, broccoli purée, horseradish emulsion, blue cheese crumb, bone marrow jus

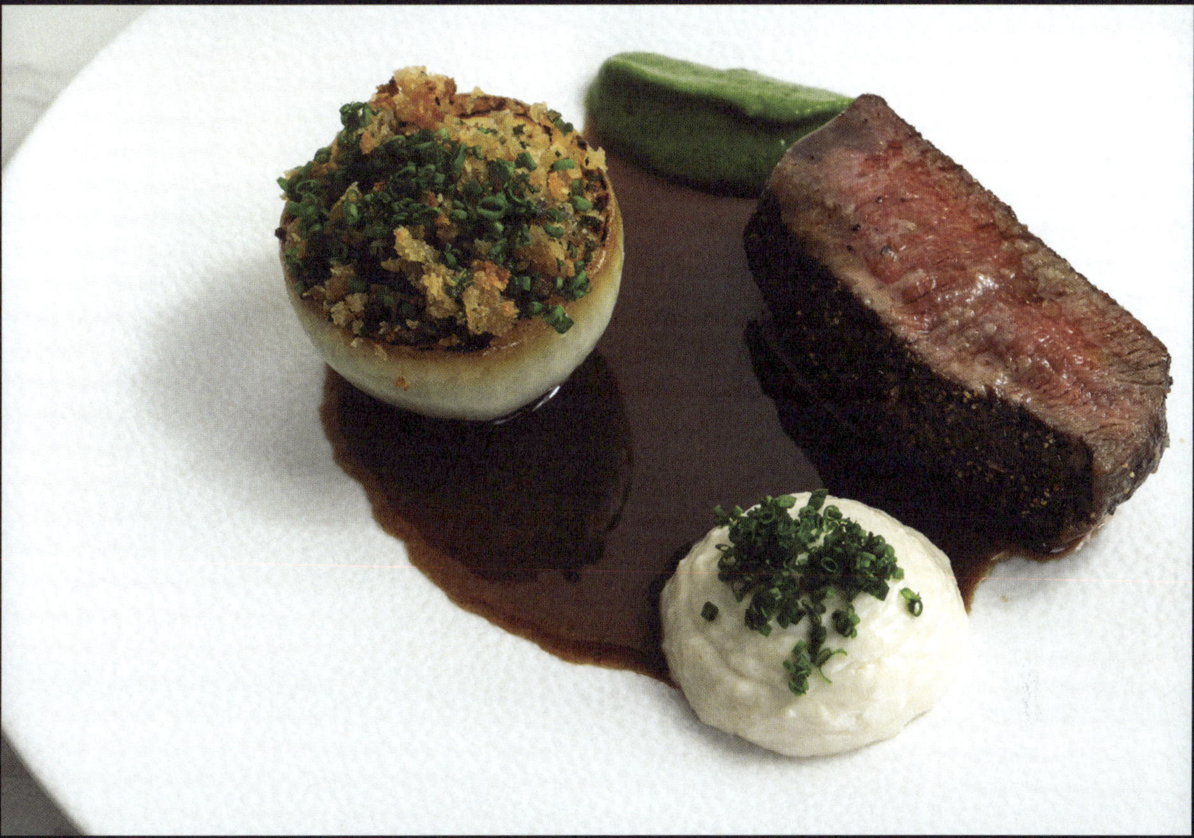

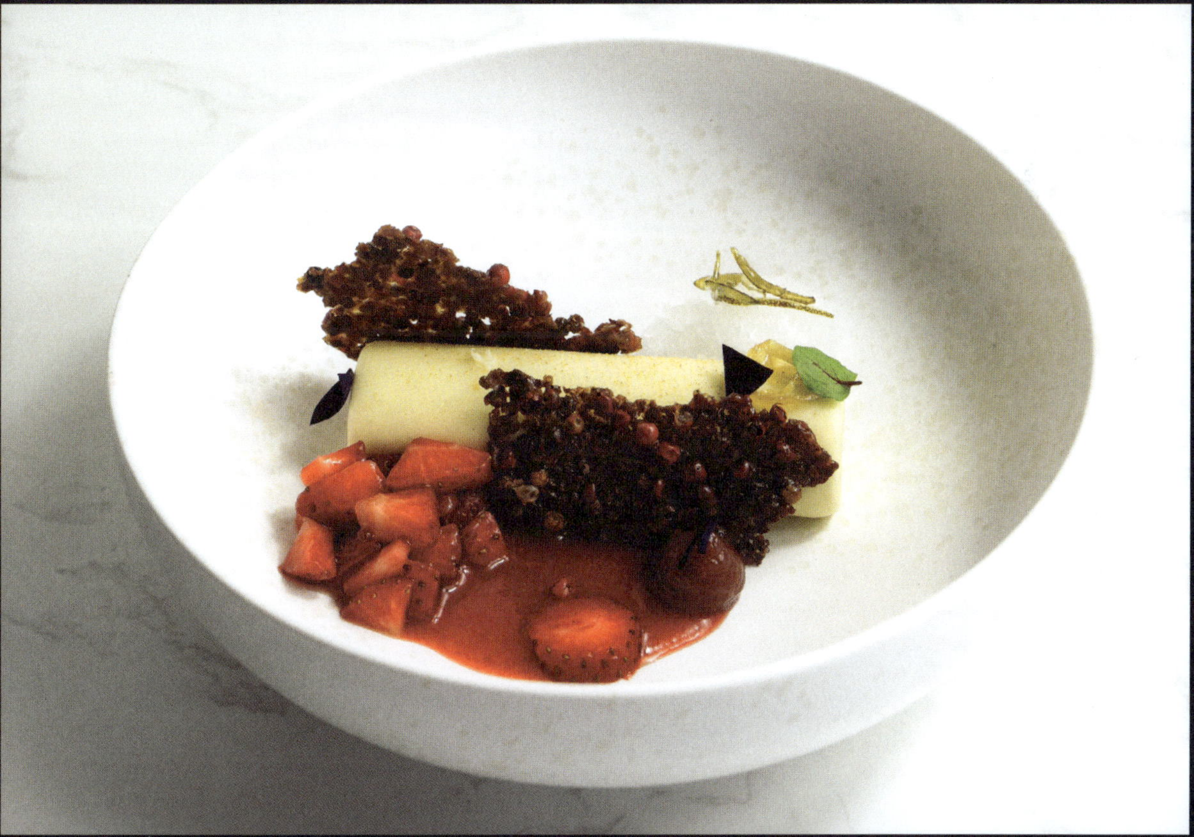

Page 29 White chocolate and ginger parfait, Jawbox granita, strawberry, pink peppercorn tuille

Scallop, chicken, pickled walnut ketchup, cauliflower, tarragon

Ingredients

Scallops

Scallops - 5

Water - 500ml

Salt - 25g

Pickled walnut ketchup

White onion - 250g. Finely diced

Dates - 40g. Soaked overnight

White wine vinegar - 25g

Dark brown sugar - 25g

Light brown sugar - 25g

Pickled walnuts - 1 jar

Roast cauliflower

Butter - 20g

Cauliflower - 1 head

Cauliflower purée

Cauliflower - 1

Full fat milk - 300ml

Butter - 30g

Chicken skin

Chicken skin - 4

Chicken butter sauce

Chicken stock - 300ml. Double reduced

Butter - 100g

Double cream - 50ml

Sherry vinegar - 1 tbsp

Tarragon oil

Picked tarragon leaves - 200g

Vegetable oil - 100g

Method

Serves 4

Scallops Remove the roe. Place the scallops in a 5% brine (500ml water, 25g fine salt dissolved) solution for 1 min.

Pickled walnut ketchup Sweat off the onions until soft and translucent. Add soaked dates, sugar and vinegar and cook for 5 mins. Bring up to heat, blitz in stand blender until smooth. Pass through fine sieve.

Roast cauliflower Remove florets from cauliflower, using only 2. Cut through the centre down the way. Place 20g of butter into a saucepan, melt until bubbling. Place the cauliflower flat side down into the pan of butter, on a medium heat. Colour the cauliflower until golden brown. Place into a preheated oven at 180°C for 3 mins.

Cauliflower purée Using the remains of the cauliflower head, chop down until a consistent small size. Melt 20g of butter in a large saucepan over a low-medium heat. Add cauliflower and soften but don't colour. Add milk until cauliflower is covered. Cook for approx. 10 mins until soft and tender. Remove liquid and add to stand blender. Add milk until desired consistency is gained while blitzing. Pass and season with fine salt and white pepper to taste.

Chicken skin Remove excess fat, spread out as thinly as possible between two sheets of greaseproof paper. Place paper with chicken skin within between two identical trays, place in the oven with a weight on top to ensure the crisp stays thin and cooks evenly. Bake at 180°C for 25 mins. Remove from paper and place onto a cold surface. Season with salt and serve.

Chicken butter sauce Boil stock, "monter" the butter into the sauce whilst continuously whisking, add cream and sherry. Important to add the butter cube by cube, whilst the stock is over a medium heat, continuously whisking to avoid it from splitting.

Tarragon oil Add into a stand blender. Take to 60°C. Pass through a muslin cloth. Place into a piping bag and hang in the freezer overnight. Remove from the freezer and discard the solidified water at the base of the bag and keep the gel like liquid.

To serve Warm the plates in the oven. Spoon the cauliflower purée onto the plate. Place the seared scallops around the plate. Dot the pickled walnut ketchup around the plate. Spoon the chicken butter sauce and drizzle the tarragon oil. Finish with shards of chicken skin and serve.

White chocolate and ginger parfait, Jawbox granita, strawberry, pink peppercorn tuille

Ingredients

Method

Serves 4

White chocolate and ginger parfait

Sugar - 150g

Water - 75ml

Egg yolks - 6

Whipping cream - 200ml

White chocolate - 200g

Fresh ginger - 30g

Gin granita

Water - 100ml

Caster sugar - 200g

Jawbox gin (or alternative) - 150ml

Fever tree tonic water - 500ml

Juiced lemon - 1

Macerated strawberries

Strawberries - 1 punnet

Sugar - 4 tbsp

Balsamic vinegar - 1 tsp

Strawberry soup

Strawberries - 1 punnet

Sugar - 2 tbsp

Balsamic vinegar - 1 tsp

Strawberry gel

Strawberry soup (above) - 200ml

Agar agar - 2g

Candied lime

Limes - 5

Caster sugar - 150g

Water - 100ml

Pink peppercorn tuille

Full fat milk - 25ml

Liquid glucose - 25g

Softened butter - 62g

Caster sugar - 75g

Crushed pink peppercorns - 40g

White chocolate and ginger parfait Whip cream to a soft peak. Melt white chocolate. Add ginger, fold through whipped cream and place to the side. Place egg yolks into a stand mixer with the whisk attachment. Whisk to combine yolks. Add water and sugar into a sauce pan and take to 121°C, using a thermometer. Pour sugar and water solution over the egg yolks while whisking on a moderate speed. Continue to whisk until the solution is completely cold. Fold together the cool egg and sugar mixture and the cream with the white chocolate and ginger. Either place into a non stick mould or roll out between cling film and roll until a cylinder shape. Allow to set before serving for two hours.

Gin granita Heat the water with the sugar for about 5 mins until dissolved. Add the remaining ingredients and pour into a freezer-proof container. Cool to room temperature, then freeze. After 1 hr, remove and whisk with a fork (or whizz in a food processor) to break up the ice crystals. Then return to the freezer. Repeat after another hour. Before serving, break up the granita with a fork to give it a softer texture. Serve topped with edible flower petals, such as violas, if you like.

Macerated strawberries Wash, hull, and slice strawberries and place into a large glass bowl. Stir in sugar and balsamic and allow to stand for 30 mins for strawberries to release their natural juices. But not so long that they begin to become mush.

Strawberry soup Roughly chop the strawberries. Place into a large mixing bowl. Toss the strawberries in the sugar and vinegar. Place into a medium size saucepan and slowly simmer for 10 – 15 mins, or until the liquid has left the strawberries. Strain over a muslin cloth and cool immediately over ice.

Strawberry gel Using the strawberry soup, place into a saucepan and boil. Vigorously whisk in the agar agar (hand blender is a good option to ensure agar agar is well incorporated). Place onto a tray and allow to cool until firm. Place into a stand blender and blitz until smooth. If smooth consistency has not been achieved add sugar syrup until a smooth fluid gel has formed.

Candied lime Peel the rind off the limes. Remove the pith with a small knife and carefully julienne into even strips. Boil and discard water keeping the limes. Repeat this process five times (this removes the bitterness of the lime). Make a sugar syrup using 100ml of water and 100g of caster sugar, keeping 50g to the side. Finally boil the sugar syrup and add the julienne of lime to the boiling sugar syrup. Remove from the sugar syrup solution and with the remaining 50g of caster sugar place the lime into the sugar and coat evenly.

Pink peppercorn tuille weigh all ingredients and combine using a whisk until smooth. Fold through the chopped pink peppercorns. Preheat oven to 175°C. Spread an even layer of the tuile mix onto a silicon sheet on an oven tray. Bake at 175°C for 10 – 12 mins. Remove from the non-stick sheet and place on a cool surface. Serve within a day.

To serve Place the parfait in the centre of the bowl. Dot the strawberry gel around the parfait. Pour the strawberry soup around the parfait to the right hand side. Place two shards of the tuille to either side of the parfait. Finally place the granita to the right hand side of the parfait and finish with candied lime. Serve immediately.

03

Grand Central
Damian Tumilty
Executive head chef

> "We use the finest local produce with fresh, high-quality ingredients that makes the food exciting and tasteful and brings out the flavour of the dishes."

The Grand Central is a Five-Star hotel in central Belfast with 300 bedrooms and two excellent restaurants. The vibrant Grand Café, which is open all day, has a laid-back appeal and focuses on casual dining. While the Seahorse is a fine dining restaurant with three sections: the restaurant itself, a lounge and a cocktail bar. Within the Seahorse there's also a high-end private dining space called the Cavern.

Grand Central Hotel offers a comprehensive dining experience including fine dining, casual dining and afternoon teas, catering for a wide range of people.

I've always wanted to be a chef since I started watching TV cooking shows such as Ready, Steady Cook. When I saw celebrity chef Rick Stein on the screen, I decided that is what I wanted to do.

I studied for a degree in culinary arts at Newry Catering College then worked in a few local places rising to chef de partie before working with Conrad Gallager at his One Michelin Star restaurant in Dublin. I moved onto the Oriel of Gilford restaurant for seven years which was awarded a Michelin Star while I was there, before opening my own place called Café Vaudeville in Belfast and, latterly, becoming executive head chef at Grand Central.

The Grand Café serves an extensive breakfast menu which includes avocado, poached egg and French toast while our all-day offerings include crispy duck salad, croque messieurs, rump of lamb and braised ox cheek all served in a casual setting.

The Seahorse Restaurant offers an excellent menu of mainly local produce that includes venison, lamb, shellfish and lobster. Caviar and Foie Gras are on offer at the Cavern for private dining.

The Grand café appeals to a lot of office workers and people hosting business meetings during the day while at night people come in for pre-theatre dinners before going onto other events. Seahorse Restaurant is more high-end with the option of a tasting menu or four-course menu.

Both venues have become very popular with local people as well as hotel guests.

I'm very proud of the food in both restaurants. We use the finest local produce with fresh, high-quality ingredients instilling a creative culture in the kitchen that makes the food exciting and tasteful and brings out the flavour of the dishes. I really want to highlight the cooking skills that goes into making our food.

Northern Ireland is a place where most chefs know each other and foster a great supportive dining culture. Belfast may be a small city, but it has one of the best food scenes and cultures of any UK city which is great for both tourists and local people.

Our customers are far more knowledgeable about food and dining than they were a few decades ago. Their expectations are far higher, and I'm delighted to say that at Grand Central Hotel, both in the Grand Café and Seahorse restaurants, we aim to satisfy those expectations.

Halibut, spinach, dulce and caviar butter sauce

Ingredients

Butter sauce

Butter - 2 tsp

Banana shallots - 2. Finely chopped

Garlic clove - 1. Finely chopped

White wine - 100ml

Veg stock - 300ml

Bay leaves - 2

Star anise - 1

Cream - 300ml

Diced butter - 50g

Spinach

Spinach - 2 large bunches. Washed and picked

Olive oil - 2 tbsp

Garlic clove - 2. Sliced

Halibut

Olive oil - 1 tbsp

Halibut - 4 x 170g fillets. Skin removed.

Butter - 2 tbsp

To serve

Dulse - 1 tsp

Trout caviar - 1 tbsp

Method

Serves 4

Butter Sauce Melt the butter in a pot over medium heat. Add the shallots and garlic, cook until translucent. Pour in the white wine and reduce by half. Add the vegetable stock and reduce again by half. Add the cream, gently simmer and reduce by half again. Pass through a fine sieve. Keep warm for service.

Spinach Sauté the garlic. Heat 2 tbsp olive oil in a large skillet on medium-high heat. Add the garlic and sauté for about 30 secs, until the garlic just begins to brown. Add the spinach to the pan, packing it down a bit with your hand, if you need to. Use a couple of spatulas (or tongs) to lift the spinach and turn it over in the pan, so you coat more of it with the olive oil and garlic. Do this a couple of times. Cover the pan and cook for 1 min. Uncover and turn the spinach over again. Cover the pan and cook for an additional min. Remove from heat and drain the excess liquid.

After 2 mins of covered cooking, the spinach should be completely wilted. Remove from heat. Drain any excess liquid from the pan. Add a little more olive oil, if you wish. Then, sprinkle with salt to taste. Serve immediately.

Halibut Heat the olive oil in a nonstick frying pan over medium heat. Season the halibut lightly, place the presentation side down in a hot pan and cook for 30 secs. Add the butter and baste the fish as it cooks until golden.

To serve Gently heat the sauce and whisk in the remaining butter slowly until emulsified. Add the dulse and the caviar and remove from the heat. Place the spinach in a bowl, top with the fish, and finish with the sauce.

< Local scallops, Thai green curry, baby bok choy

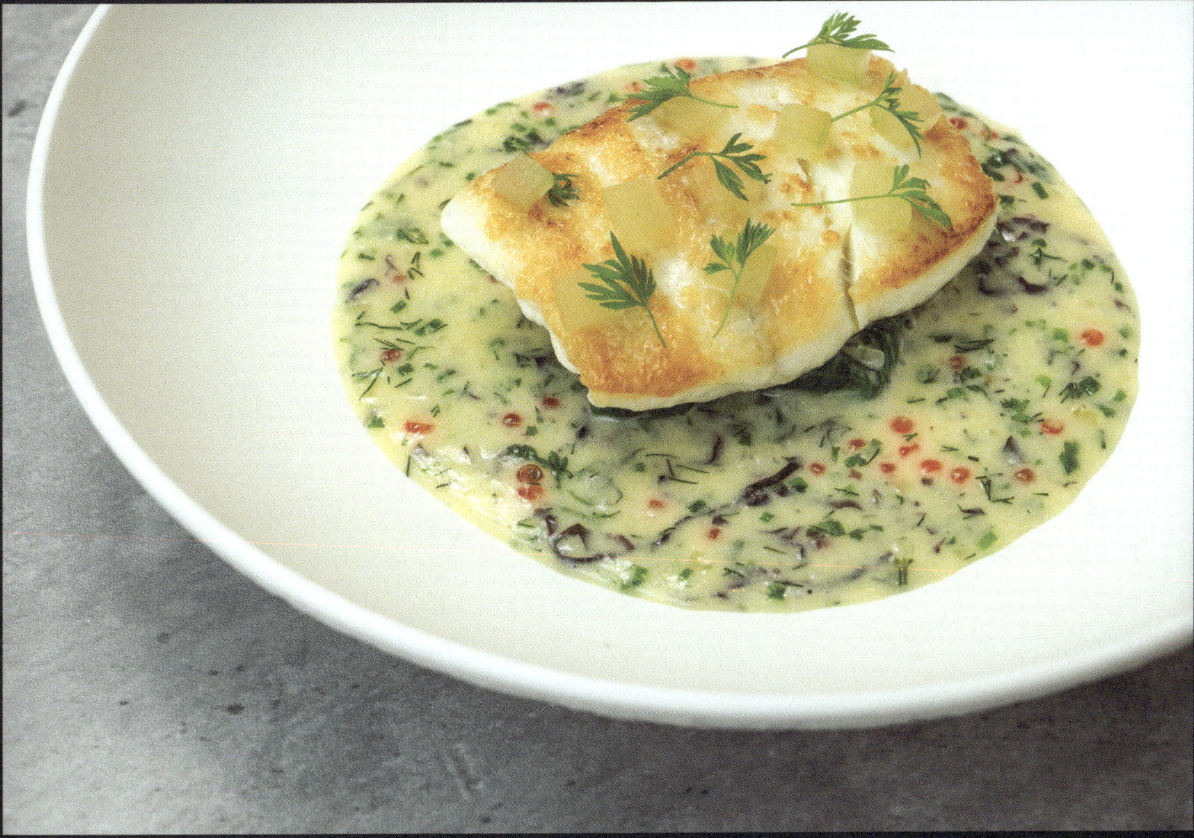

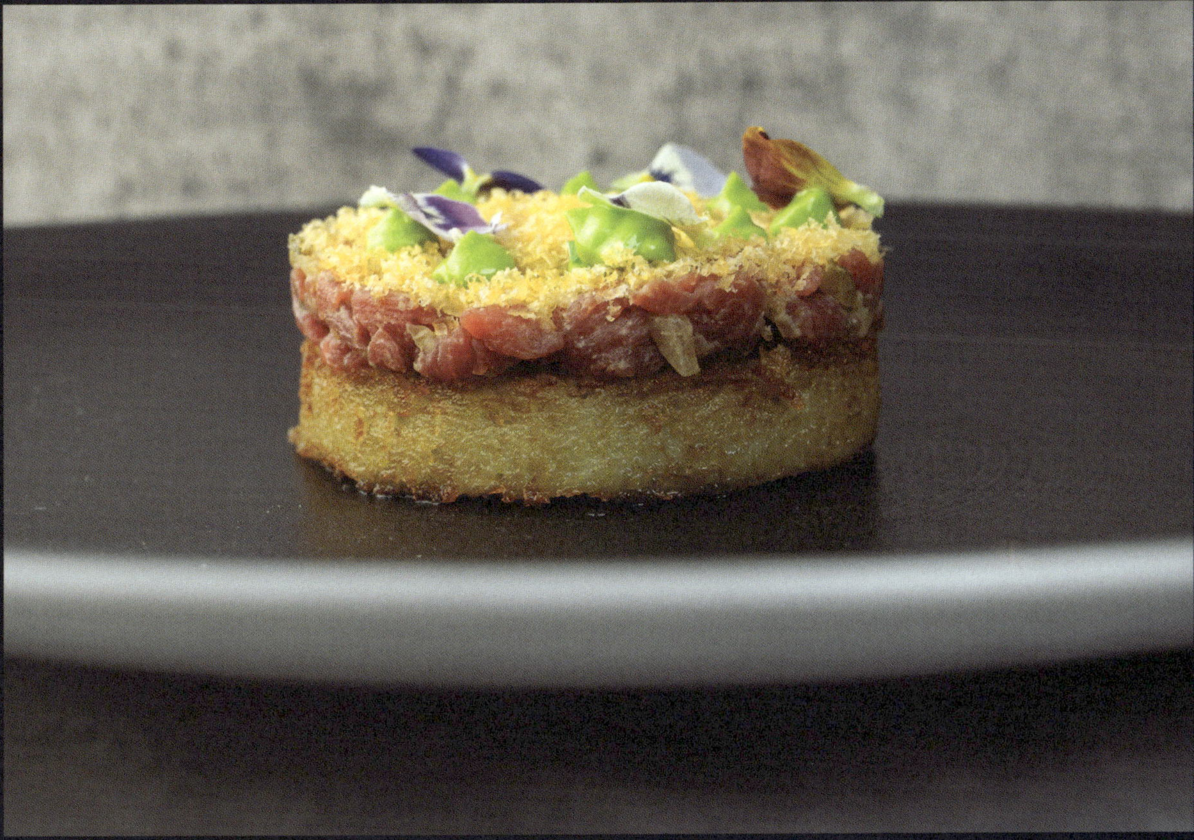

Page 36 Irish angus beef tartar, broad beans, potato roster, wild garlic emulsion

Irish moiled beef, roast onion, braised cheek and peppercorn cream

Ingredients

The beef

Dry aged Irish moiled sirloin steaks - 2 x 300g

Beef cheek - To be done the day before

Beef cheek - 500g

Water - 1l

Salt - 100g

Brown sugar - 50g

Red wine vinegar - 50g

Red wine - 1 glass

Green peppercorn cream

Shallots - 4

Garlic - 2 cloves

Thyme - 2 sprigs

Brandy - 200ml

Brined green peppercorns - 4 tbsp

Beef stock - 1l

Double cream - 200ml

Method

Beef cheek Preheat the oven to 150°C. Add some oil, then carefully colour the cheek until caramelised. Remove the cheek and deglaze with red wine. Then add the stock and place the cheek back into the pan.

Cover with baking paper and place the cheek into the oven and cook 4 – 5 hrs until tender. Once cooked leave to cool. Meanwhile transfer all the cooking juices to a pan and start to reduce them slowly. Pick the rested beef into nice pieces. Fold through the reduced cooking liquor – season, and add the vinegar. Cool and place in the fridge until ready to use.

Stuffed onions Preheat the oven to 180°C. Place the onions on a tray. Bake for 30 – 45 mins until soft, then leave to cool.

Carefully peel the onions and cut in half. When you are ready to serve remove the inside of the oven onion to leave 3 outer layers. Reheat the beef cheek. Spoon this into the onion skin.

Moiled beef Heat a large frying pan over a high heat until smoking. Season the steaks heavily with salt and pepper, then place them in the hot pan and sear on each side. Remove from the pan and leave to rest.

Green peppercorn cream Slowly caramelise the shallots and garlic. Then add peppercorns, reserving 1 tbsp. Deglaze with the brandy, reserving 20ml for later. Add the beef stock – reduce by half. Add the double cream – bring to the boil. Pass through a strainer. Add the remaining brandy and peppercorns. Season with salt to taste.

To serve Place roast onion on the plate. Halve the sirloin, and finish with green peppercorn cream.

< Irish moiled beef, roast onion, braised cheek and peppercorn cream

Page 37 Clandeboye cheesecake, Clandeboye yogurt, Armagh strawberry sorbet, elderflower

Irish angus beef tartar, broad beans, potato roster, wild garlic emulsion

Ingredients

Tartar mix

Beef fillet - 200g. Finely chopped

Baby capers - 1 tbsp. Roughly chopped

Shallot - 1. Finely diced

Cornichons - 3. Finely diced

Worcestershire sauce - 1 tsp

Dijon mustard - 2 tbsp. Use bind ingredients

Wild garlic emulsion

Egg yolks - 40g

Chardonnay vinegar - 15g

Vegetable oil - 100g

Wild garlic oil - 75g

Dijon mustard - 2g

Gelespessa - 2g

Potato Rosti

Rooster potatoes - 1kg. Grated

Beef fat - 200g

Salt - 20g

Method

Serves 4

Tartar mix Combine all ingredients in a mixing bowl.

Wild garlic emulsion Place the egg yolks, chardonnay vinegar, and Dijon mustard into a blender. Begin blending on medium speed, then slowly drizzle in the vegetable oil followed by the wild garlic oil, ensuring a steady emulsion forms. Once the mixture thickens to a mayonnaise consistency, add the gelespessa and blend briefly to fully incorporate. Adjust seasoning to taste, if desired.

Potato Rosti In a pot, gently heat the beef fat until fully melted. Peel the rooster potatoes and grate them using a coarse grater. In a large mixing bowl, combine the grated potatoes with the melted beef fat and salt. Mix thoroughly to ensure even coating. Transfer the mixture to a lined or greased tray, pressing it down evenly. Bake in the preheated oven for 1 hour and 30 mins.
Allow to cool completely before slicing or portioning.

To Serve Cut the potato out with a cutter and deep fry at 180°C until crispy. Mix the tartar mix and place on top of the rosti. Finish with the wild garlic mayonnaise .

Clandeboye cheesecake. Clandeboye yogurt, Armagh strawberry sorbet, elderflower

Ingredients

Cheesecake mix

Labneh - 250g

Double cream - 150ml

Elderflower essence - 5ml

Vanilla pod - Seeds only

Orange - 1. Zest

Caster sugar - 200g

Tahini crumb

Unsalted butter - 100g

Plain flour - 100g

Tahini - 100g

Strawberry sorbet

Large lemons - 3. 1 seeded and Roughly chopped. The others juiced

Granulated sugar - 396g

Strawberries - 2 pounds. Hulled

Method

Cheesecake mix Combine all the ingredients in a mixing bowl.

Tahini crumb Combine all the ingredients in a mixing bowl.

Strawberry sorbet Place the chopped lemon and sugar in a food processor and pulse until combined. Transfer to a bowl. Alternatively, pulse with a blender or immersion blender in a large bowl.

Purée the strawberries in a food processor (or using one of the alternatives listed above) and add to the lemon mixture, along with the juice of 1 lemon. Taste and add more juice as desired. The lemon flavour should be intense but should not overpower the strawberries.

Pour the mixture into an ice cream machine and churn until frozen. Alternatively, pour into a shallow dish and freeze, stirring every half hour or so, until firm and scoopable. Serve right away or cover and freeze. For the best texture and flavour, eat within a few days. If frozen too hard, let it soften for 10 mins or until just soft enough to scoop.

To serve Pipe the cheesecake mixture into a bowl or glass. Top with tahini crumb and a scoop of sorbet.

04

Lo & Slo
Emily McCorkell
Resident caterer
and owner

Lo & Slo BBQ is an immersive and interactive experience where people participate in our barbecue workshops. Here they cook wonderful food with our custom range of award-winning barbecue sauces based on two family recipes, before eating and celebrating together within the beautiful Brook Hall Estate in Derry.

My husband and I started Lo & Slo BBQ after successful stints at food festivals and trading from a street food trailer during lockdown. We expanded our product range and began our barbecue school in 2024.

People visibly relax when they come to our barbecues because they're interacting with real food, which is made from hyper-local ingredients. They are working with and eating fresh and healthy produce while connecting with each other. We're hopefully inspiring and empowering them to make good food choices.

Our cookery classes and catering are in an ancient garden on the estate which is well over 400 years old. We supply our customers with the tools, skills and knowledge to cook better at home without artificial ingredients using a seasonal and fresh menu from local producers.

Our tagline is "Taste the Landscape" and this is what our customers experience as they'll be eating beef which comes from just 30 miles up the road. The steaks they cook are gamey and full of flavour from all-year round grass-fed wild cows, farmed ethically and humanely. We're proud of our suppliers and encourage them to come to the site and talk to our customers. In the barbecue workshops, the participants are taught how to cook their tomahawk steaks directly on the coals. We give away our recipes which is a

vital part of our ethos about being eco-friendly and sustainable.

Most of our customers are in their mid-30s to mid-50s. Many are FIT or Fully Independent travellers, seeking more adventurous cooking, wanting to hear the story behind the food they're eating and the land it comes from. Before cooking begins, we take them on a tour of the garden and explain that the farm on the estate is carbon positive and part of a series of innovative lighthouse farms across Europe.

After the workshops people take their food to our large forty-seat food court where they sit around log tables which encourages communication and trust, promoting the idea that food is a vehicle for connection, culture and healing. Our customers leave feeling they've participated in something positive and engaging.

Northern Ireland is a very collaborative place to work and operate, especially in food, agriculture and hospitality. People support each other. You're virtually tripping over producers who are excellent, and all have stories to tell. I'm delighted to know the names of all the farmers who supply us and their children. It's a great place. I love it. Anywhere you go in Northern Ireland is cool and I'm thrilled that Lo and Slo BBQ has become such an innovative and important part in developing a sustainable culinary landscape.

"People visibly relax when they come to our barbecues because they're interacting with real food... They are working with and eating fresh and healthy produce while connecting with each other."

Creamy burrata with lemon and charred blackberries

Ingredients

Burrata

Burrata - 450g. Drained weight

Lemon - 1. Zest

Extra virgin olive oil - 30ml

Red chilli flakes - 2g

Flaky sea salt and cracked black pepper - To taste

Fresh wood sorrel - A few sprigs

Blackberries

Fresh blackberries - 200g

To serve

Your favourite bread, toasted and warm

Method

Serves 4

Prepare a medium-hot fire or grill. Place the blackberries in a fireproof pan or directly on a grill grate. Cook over direct heat for 30 – 60 secs, just until they begin to blister and soften. Remove from heat.

Place the burrata on a serving platter and gently tear it open. Drizzle with olive oil and sprinkle with chilli flakes, sea salt, and cracked black pepper.

Spoon the charred blackberries over the burrata, allowing their juices to mingle with the cheese. Finish with fresh lemon zest and a few sprigs of wood sorrel.

Serve immediately with your favourite warm, toasted bread for scooping.

< Creamy burrata with lemon and charred blackberries

Page 44 Firepit mussels with whiskey herb dressing

Dirty tomahawks with hispi cabbage and butter-braised potatoes

Ingredients

Tomahawks

Tomahawk steaks - 2. Thick-cut, bone-in. Approx. 1kg each, at least 1 inch thick

Flaky sea salt

Chilli flakes

Herby dressing

Fresh parsley - 20g. Finely chopped

Fresh basil - 20g. Finely chopped

Salt - A pinch

Cracked black pepper - To taste

Honey - 25g

Rapeseed oil - 15ml

Lemon - 1. Zest

Apple cider vinegar - 55ml

Hispi cabbage

Pointed (hispi) cabbage - 1. Quartered

Rapeseed oil - 30ml

Fermented hot honey - 25g

A splash of whiskey

Apple cider vinegar - 15ml

Lemon - 1/2. Zest

Cracked black pepper - To taste

Sea salt flakes

Butter-braised potatoes

Baby potatoes - 600g

Butter - 150g

Extra virgin olive oil - 60ml

Flaky sea salt

Chilli flakes

Method

Serves 4

Start with the potatoes In a fireproof pan, melt the butter and oil directly over the coals or on a grill rack. Add the potatoes, flaky sea salt and chilli flakes. Cover with a lid or foil and cook slowly for 20 – 25 mins, shaking occasionally to ensure even browning. The potatoes should become tender and coated in rich, golden fat.

Prepare the cabbage Place the quartered hispi cabbage on the cooler side of the grill and allow it to smoke slowly until tender – about 20 – 25 mins. Once softened, move it over direct flame to char the edges. Remove, chop roughly, and toss in the vinaigrette. Set back over warm coals in a heatproof dish until ready to serve.

Make the herby dressing Whisk together the vinegar, honey, and oil until fully incorporated. Stir in the parsley, basil, lemon zest, a pinch of salt, and cracked black pepper. Set aside.

Cook the tomahawks last Bring steaks to room temperature and prepare a hot, even bed of coals. Choose a spot with solid, even ember coverage – maximum surface contact is key. Avoid large gaps that can cause uneven cooking or burning.

Place the steaks directly onto the coals ('dirty style') and cook for 10 – 15 mins, or until the internal temperature reaches around 39°C. Flip the steaks and continue cooking. Remove from the coals when they are 3 – 4°C below your desired doneness:
Rare: 49–52°C / Medium rare: 53–57°C

To serve Slice the rested tomahawks and spoon over the herby dressing. Plate alongside the butter-braised potatoes and smoky, fire-charred cabbage.

Firepit mussels with whiskey herb dressing

Ingredients

Mussels

Fresh mussels - 1kg. Cleaned and debearded

Whiskey herb dressing

Rapeseed oil - 30ml

Apple cider vinegar - 15ml

Whiskey - 15ml

Fermented hot honey - 10g

Small shallot - 1. Finely diced

Garlic - 1 clove. Finely minced

Fresh parsley - 20g. Finely chopped

Fresh basil - 20g. Finely chopped

Red chilli - 1 small. Finely diced

Lemon - 1. Zest and juice

**Cracked black pepper and sea salt
-** To taste

To serve

**Stout wheaten bread or a crusty loaf
-** Fire-toasted

Method

Serves 4

Choose clean, fresh mussels. Remove any beards and discard any that are broken or remain open when tapped.

First, make the whiskey herb dressing. Whisk together the apple cider vinegar, fermented hot honey, and rapeseed oil until combined. Stir in the parsley, basil, shallot, garlic, red chilli, lemon zest and juice. Season to taste with cracked black pepper and sea salt. Set aside.

Prepare a medium-hot fire with a strong, steady flame. Place the mussels in a metal wire basket or grill-safe tray.

Hold the basket directly over the flames, gently shaking every 20 – 30 secs to avoid shell scorching. The mussels will begin to open within 2 – 3 mins.

Once opened fully and the mussels are an opaque peachy colour, remove immediately from the heat and toss with the whiskey herb dressing while still hot, coating them thoroughly.

Serve at once with fire-toasted stout wheaten bread or a crusty loaf for dipping.

Smoked brioche pudding with seasonal fruit

Ingredients

Pudding

Croissants or slices of brioche - 3 – 4 or 450g. Roughly torn

Whole milk - 300ml

Double cream - 150ml

Eggs - 2

Sugar - 100g

Vanilla extract - 4ml

Ground cinnamon - 3g. Optional

Seasonal fruit (e.g. rhubarb, berries, or stone fruit) - 150g. Slightly charred and chopped

To finish

Butter - for greasing

Honey or whiskey cream liquor - To taste. Optional

Method

Serves 4

Butter a cast iron pan or baking dish. Tear croissants or brioche into pieces and scatter in the pan.

Lightly soften the chopped seasonal fruit (such as rhubarb) over an open flame or hot grill until just beginning to break down. Scatter the softened fruit over the bread.

In a bowl, whisk together the eggs, milk, cream, sugar, vanilla, and cinnamon. Pour over the bread and fruit, pressing down gently so everything is well soaked.

Set the mixture aside to rest for 10 mins to allow the custard to absorb fully.

Cover the dish tightly with foil and bake over indirect heat on the fire – or in a preheated oven at 180°C for about 40 mins, or until the internal temperature reaches 71°C. Keeping it covered helps prevent excessive smoke from overwhelming the pudding, which can lead to bitterness.

Uncover for the final 10 mins to crisp the top slightly.

Let cool briefly before serving with a drizzle of honey or a splash of whiskey cream, if desired.

05 La Bottega
Francesco Iaquinta/ Fabrizio Caramia
Owner/head chef

Fabrizio Caramia, head chef

"A little slice of Italy abroad."

La Bottega is an authentic Italian restaurant and café situated on the bustling Lisburn Road, part of the "Golden Mile" in Belfast. It's a little slice of Italy abroad and when you step into La Bottega, Francesco and Fabrizio want you to feel immersed in Italian cuisine, culture and surroundings.

Francesco has worked in hospitality since he was fifteen, studying in Bologna and working in some of the finest restaurants there, including Michelin Starred ones. Arriving in Belfast eleven years ago he opened La Bottega in 2021 initially as a café and mini market selling deli cuts and charcuterie and cheese boards, before opening the restaurant kitchen in 2023.

Fabrizio, born in Puglia (southern Italy), moved to Milan at a young age where he attended Hospitality school for five years. After receiving his diploma, he worked in one of the city's oldest restaurants for three years. In 2014 he came to London and worked in a range of high-end fine dining Rosette restaurants, before coming to Belfast and working with Francesco at La Bottega.

Everything about La Bottega is authentically Italian: the food, the wine, the vibe, the colours, even the crockery! It's the only restaurant in the whole of Ireland to be given the Ospitalita Italiana award from the Italian Chamber of Commerce bestowed on restaurants that guarantee the quality and hospitality standards to promote Italian food and wine culture.

Francesco and Fabrizio's passion is to educate people about authentic Italian cuisine. Fabrizio uses simple ingredients to transform traditional dishes such as lasagna, parmigiana, bruschetta or pappardelle into delicious dishes imbued with beautiful flavours as if they had been cooked back in Italy.

To highlight the amazing variety of Italian food, La Bottega hosts a "Regional Night" event which focuses on one region of Italy and spotlights its distinctive food and wine offerings. There is also a regular Jazz Night held in the upstairs section of the restaurant while the work of local Italian artists is on display downstairs.

La Bottega has developed a regular, loyal and discerning customer base who appreciate the whole and unique experience.

Francesco is really proud of his staff "without them there would be nothing."

In addition to the Ospitalita Italiana award, La Bottega has also won Best Italian Restaurant in Ireland Award in 2024 from Yes Chef Magazine and Best Wine Experience in the Irish Restaurant Awards in 2023. The restaurant has an extensive list of great Italian wines.

Francesco and Fabrizio know that people in Northern Ireland love their food but are also keen to experiment and expand their horizons. At La Bottega they want people to feel like they are dining at home. "The people we serve at La Bottega are our guests, not just customers."

Tagliolini, ricotta, smoked salmon and salmon roe

Ingredients

Pasta dough

00 flour - 300g

Egg yolks - 3

Eggs - 1

Extra virgin olive oil - 10ml

Fine sea salt - 5g

Salmon and ricotta mousse

Sliced smoked salmon - 200g

Ricotta - 350g

Double cream - 400ml

Fresh dill - 20g

Garnish

Salmon roe - 40g

Lemons - 2. Zest

Method

Serves 4

Pasta dough Pour the flour on a table and make a well at the center of it. Slowly incorporate the eggs with the help of a fork. Add the oil and salt and work until the dough becomes smooth to touch. Let rest for at least 30 mins. Cut the dough in 4 pieces and gradually, start to roll it with the help of a pasta machine. Once the preferred thickness is achieved, use the pasta machine attachment to shape your tagliolini, or just use your knife to thinly slice the folded pasta sheets.

Salmon and ricotta mousse Remove the stalk from the dill and roughly chop with the smoked salmon. Mix everything in a bowl with ricotta and the cream.

To serve Gently heat up the salmon mousse in a pan. Meanwhile cook the tagliolini in salted water for 2– 3 mins. Toss the pasta in the pan and, with some pasta water, amalgamate all together. Plate the pasta in a warm plate, top with some salmon roe and zest some fresh lemon on top of everything.

< Tagliolini, ricotta, smoked salmone and salmon roe

Page 52 Butter poached langoustines, pickled fennel, blood orange purée, bisque foam

Lamb rump, sautéed globe artichokes, wild garlic pesto, salted ricotta

Ingredients

Lamb rumps - 4. 8oz trimmed

Wild garlic pesto

Wild garlic leaves - 150g. Washed
Extra virgin olive oil - 90ml
Flat leaf parsley - 120. Picked
Parmigiano reggiano - 150g. Grated
Pistachio - 20g. Toasted

Sautéed globe artichokes

Globe artichokes - 3
Cherry tomatoes - 300g. Sliced
Lemon - 1

Lamb jus

Lamb bones - 500g
White onion - 1
Large carrot - 1
Celery - 4 sticks
Rosemary - 3 sprigs
Thyme - 4 sprigs
Garlic cloves - 2. Crushed
Red wine - 50ml
Tomato paste - 15g

Garnish

Salted ricotta - 40g. Shaved

Method

Serves 4

Lamb jus Place the bones in a tray and roast them in the oven for 200°C for about 30 mins, or until dark brown colour. In the meantime, roughly chop your vegetable and roast them in a tall pot. Once ready add the bones into the pot, evaporate the red wine and add the rest of the ingredients. Cover with cold water and gently boil for at least 4 hrs. Strain the liquid and reduce to a thick consistency on low heat. Remember to skim the fat during the process.

Wild garlic pesto Blanche the wild garlic leaves in boiling water for 30 secs, quickly cool down in ice water. Squeeze the leaves and place the rest of the ingredients in a food processor, leaving the oil on the side. Pulse until coarse texture and slowly incorporate the oil to the mix. Leave in the fridge.

Lamb rump Score the top fat and generously season with salt and pepper. Rub the meat with vegetable oil and sear each side on a hot pan. Finish in the oven at 175°C for 7 – 8 mins for a pink result. Let it rest on rack for 2 mins and carve going against the meat fibers.

Sautée globe artichokes Clean the artichokes peeling the outer leaves until you reach the softer and lighter colored ones. Trim 3 inches from the bottom of the stem and peel it until you reach the white coloured core. Slice the flower in half and, with the help of a spoon, remove the "beard" at the center of the artichoke. Rub a slice of lemon all over it to avoid oxidation. Slice into wedges and boil for about 20 – 30 mins, or until the outer leaf is soft. Splash some olive oil in a pan and sautee the artichokes until both sides are brown. Add the sliced tomatoes and cook for a couple of minutes.

To serve With the help of a ring, make a base of pesto on a warm plate. Place the sauteed artichokes at the center and the sliced lamb on top of it. Sprinkle with shaved salted ricotta and the warm jus.

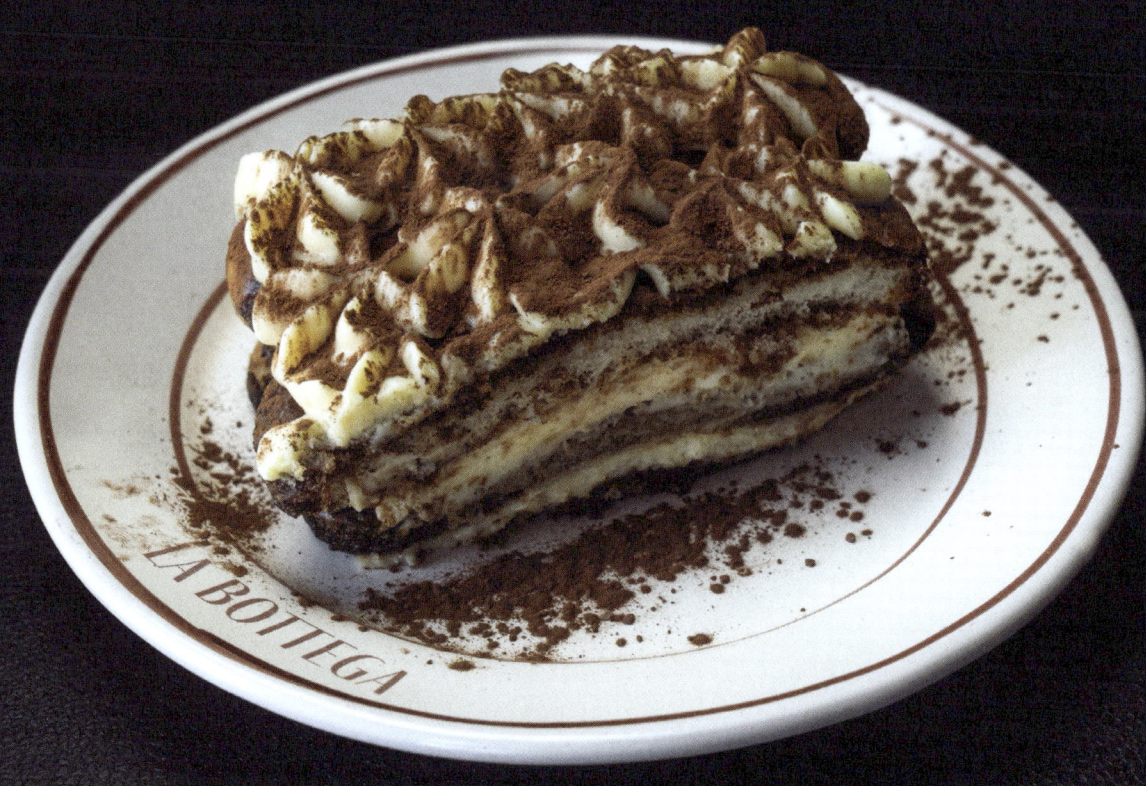

< Lamb rump, sautéed globe artichokes, wild garlic pesto, salted ricotta

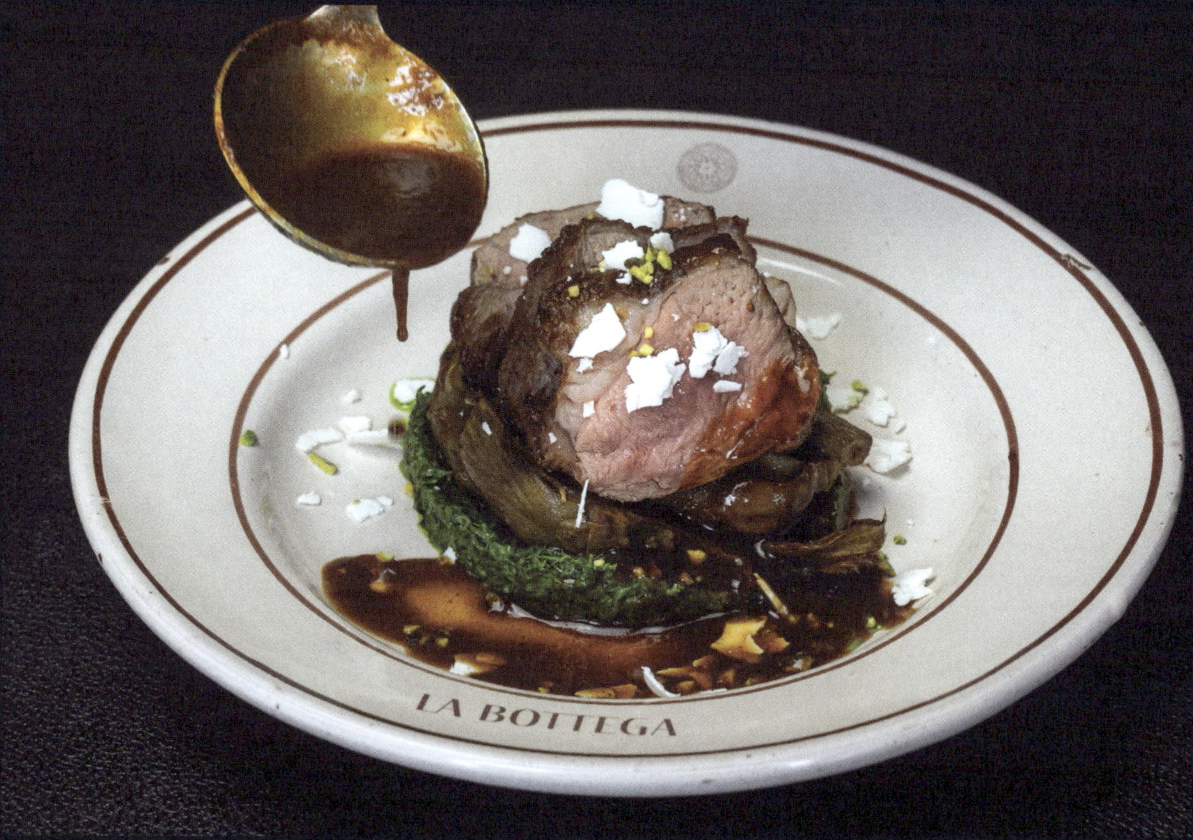
LA BOTTEGA

LA BOTTEGA

Page 53 Tiramisú

Butter poached langoustines, pickled fennel, blood orange purée, bisque foam

Ingredients

Butter poached langoustines

Langoustines - 8. Cleaned and deveined

Butter - 300g

Bisque foam

Shellfish bisque - 200ml

Whipping cream - 400ml

Lemon - 1/2. Juice

Salt

Xanthan gum - 0.2g. Optional

Orange pickled fennel

Fennel - 2 bulbs

Caster sugar - 150g

White wine vinegar - 300ml

Garlic - 1 clove. Crushed

Orange - 1. Sliced in half

Rosemary - 2 sprigs

Red chilli - 1. Split in half

Blood orange purée

Blood oranges - 2. Scored

Caster sugar - 160g

Sherry vinegar - 30ml

Water - 20ml

Method

Butter poached langoustines Melt the butter in a small pot and keep at roughly 75°C, or just under simmering point. Place the langoustine inside, making sure they are completely covered. Let steep for about 4 mins, depending on the size.

Bisque foam Reduce the shellfish bisque to roughly 20g, or until paste consistency. Lower the heat when it starts to thicken and keep whisking avoiding catching the bottom of the pan. Add the cream, the lemon juice, salt and xanthan gum (if available), and bring to boil while mixing it. Pass the liquid through a fine sieve and fill a cream whipper with it. Keep in hot water for best results.

Orange pickled fennel Trim the fennel tops and thinly slice the fennel bulb and place in a solution of water and lemon to avoid oxidation. Meanwhile, place the rest of the ingredients in a pot and bring to boil. Drain the shaved fennel. Place it in a container and pour over the hot pickled liquid making sure it is completely covered.

Blood orange purée Vertically score the oranges and boil them 7 times from cold water each time. This removes the tartness of the pith. Roughly chop them once cooked and set aside. In a pot, add sugar and water and let it caramelize to a dark brown colour. Carefully splash in the sherry vinegar, add the chopped oranges and cook on low heat for 10 – 15 mins. Blitz in a food processor at high speed and pass through a fine sieve

To serve Pat the pickled fennel and gently form a ball. Place the warm langoustine on top of it. Have fun with the orange purée and the warm bisque foam. Garnish with some fresh dill.

Tiramisú

Ingredients

Mascarpone mix

Eggs yolks - 6

Caster sugar - 250g

Mascarpone - 500g. Firm

Tiramisú

Ladyfinger biscuits - 30

Coffee - 150ml. Room temperature

Cocoa powder

Method

Serves 4

Mascarpone mix In a stand mixer bowl, place the eggs yolk and the sugar, and whisk at full speed for 7 mins. Add all the mascarpone at once and whisk again for a further 3 mins. Place in the fridge.

Tiramisú Dip the individual biscuits in coffee for a couple of seconds and start laying it in a small tray, making sure they are as close as possible and cover the whole surface. Pour some of the mascarpone mix and, with the help of a spatula, spread it equally. Repeat this process for every layer. Heavily dust with cocoa powder and keep refrigerated.

06 Lough Erne Resort
Gareth Byrne
General manager

Lough Erne Resort nestles on a private 600-acre peninsula within the Fermanagh Lakelands with 120 rooms and 25 self-catering luxury lodges. The resort, which opened in 2007, was awarded 'Hotel of the Year 2024' by Licensed Catering and News and rated by the Irish Independent as among the best hotels in Ireland. The Resort boasts two championship golf courses, a renowned Thai Spa, and four restaurants, one of which is the Catalina Restaurant. Currently, the Resort employs more than 300 staff, most of whom are from the local area.

I'm from Newcastle, County Down and graduated in Hotel & Tourism from Ulster University. I've worked for 25 years within the hospitality industry, including at luxury hotels such as The Fitzwilliam Hotel in Belfast and The Kensington, London. More recently, I was General Manager of the Duke of Richmond Hotel.

Lough Erne Resort offers a wide and diverse range of food and drink across four restaurants:

Castle Hume, attached to Castle Hume Golf Club offers a relaxing atmosphere with a classic Clubhouse menu and is very popular with our guests.

Our Loughside Grill offers exceptional steak options with recently introduced international interpretations of Irish 'staple' dishes.

The Blaney Bar offers an informal dining option within the main hotel building. It serves guest favourites like Smoked Haddock and Salmon Chowder, our famous Blaney Burger and our much-loved Lisdergan Daube of Beef. Centred on good old fashioned Fermanagh hospitality, our Blaney menu has been described as a love letter to traditional dishes passed down through the generations, accompanied by an impressive drinks' menu with the best in local craft beers and whiskies.

Our signature Catalina fine dining restaurant has a superb culinary team who work with trusted local suppliers to ensure our menus evolve with the seasons and focus on getting the most from locally produced food. The Catalina has earned a reputation as one of the best dining experiences on the island with top quality food underpinned by attentive but unobtrusive service.

Throughout the resort there is a range of vegetarian options.

The resort's dining excellence is founded on local ingredients with solid provenance, premium quality and incredible flavour. Whilst solidly Irish in our emphasis we encourage our chefs to express their individual interpretations of our dishes by incorporating the odd surprise or two.

Our culinary team has been involved in many major occasions, none more so than the 39th G8 Summit held at the resort in 2013. To cook for Presidents, Prime Ministers and other world dignitaries was an amazing privilege. It emphasised how wonderful Irish produce is as our distinguished guests were blown away with the quality of the ingredients and the dishes created by our team.

Ireland has an array of worldclass dining talent, and Lough Erne Resort is proud to showcase the best Irish ingredients, carefully prepared by our creative and talented team and enjoyed by our local, national and international guests. As someone once said, if you love what you do, you'll never work a day in your life!

"The resort's dining excellence is founded on local ingredients with solid provenance, premium quality and incredible flavour."

Gareth Byrne and Adam Milliken, Lough Erne Resort

Curried cauliflower purée and scallops

Ingredients

Scallops - 8. 40g

Cauliflower purée

Cauliflower - 1 head

Medium curry powder - 1 tbsp

White onion - 120g. Chopped

Chardonnay white wine - 75ml

Dijon mustard - 1/2 tbsp

Parsley - Small bunch

Olive oil - 2 tbsp

Curry oil

Olive oil - 150ml

Garlic - 5 cloves

Shallots - 55g. Diced

Medium curry powder - 2 tbsp

Red chillies - 30g. Chopped

Golden raisin - 1/2 tbsp

Method

Serves 4

For the purée Roughly chop Cauliflower and lightly roast off with onions in olive oil. Add chardonnay and reduce to one third. Add parsley, curry powder and Dijon Mustard and allow to cook for 5 mins. Take off the heat and blitz for 5 mins.

For the curry oil Sautée chilies, shallot and garlic on a low heat with 5ml of oil. Once soft to touch add curry powder. Add the remaining oil and bring to 63°C. Add to metal mixing bowl and blitz until smooth. Pass through a Shinwa and add raisins to soak.

For the scallops Sear Scallops on both sides and cook for 3 mins on the pan. Then remove and allow to rest for 1 min and serve.

To serve Use the remaining cauliflower and lightly soften in a pan until brown. Add raisins and remove from the heat. Use the purée 30g on each plate and add the scallops. Place cauliflower and raisins beside the scallop and finish with a drizzle of oil.

< Curried cauliflower purée and scallops

Page 60 Chicken parfait

Irish pan seared hake

Ingredients

Hake fillet - 500g
Thyme - 1 stalk
Blackberry purée - 200ml
Agar - 3g
Clams and prawn - 50g
Goats bridge trout roe - 10g
Samphire - 20g
Butter - 100g

Method

Serves 2

To create the Blackberry purée place the blackberries and thyme in a pot and bring to a simmer. When simmering add the agar and whisk in until dissolved. Remove from the heat and allow to cool.

Once cooled blitz in a mixer until smooth (dress the plate with gel). Place the hake skin side down on a hot pan and cook for 6 mins.

Cook the clams and prawn in butter for roughly 3 mins. With a small amount of butter cook off the samphire. Strain butter off and serve. Finish by adding some goats bridge trout roe.

< Irish pan seared hake

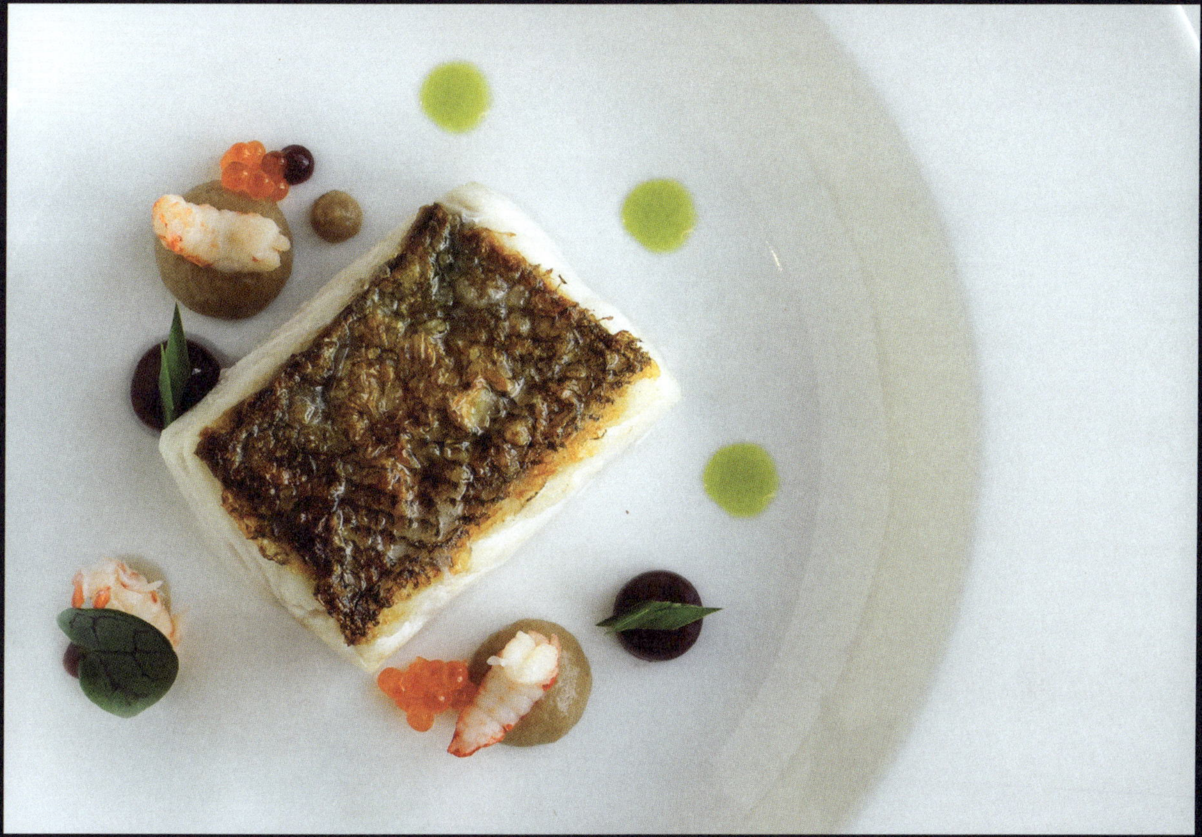

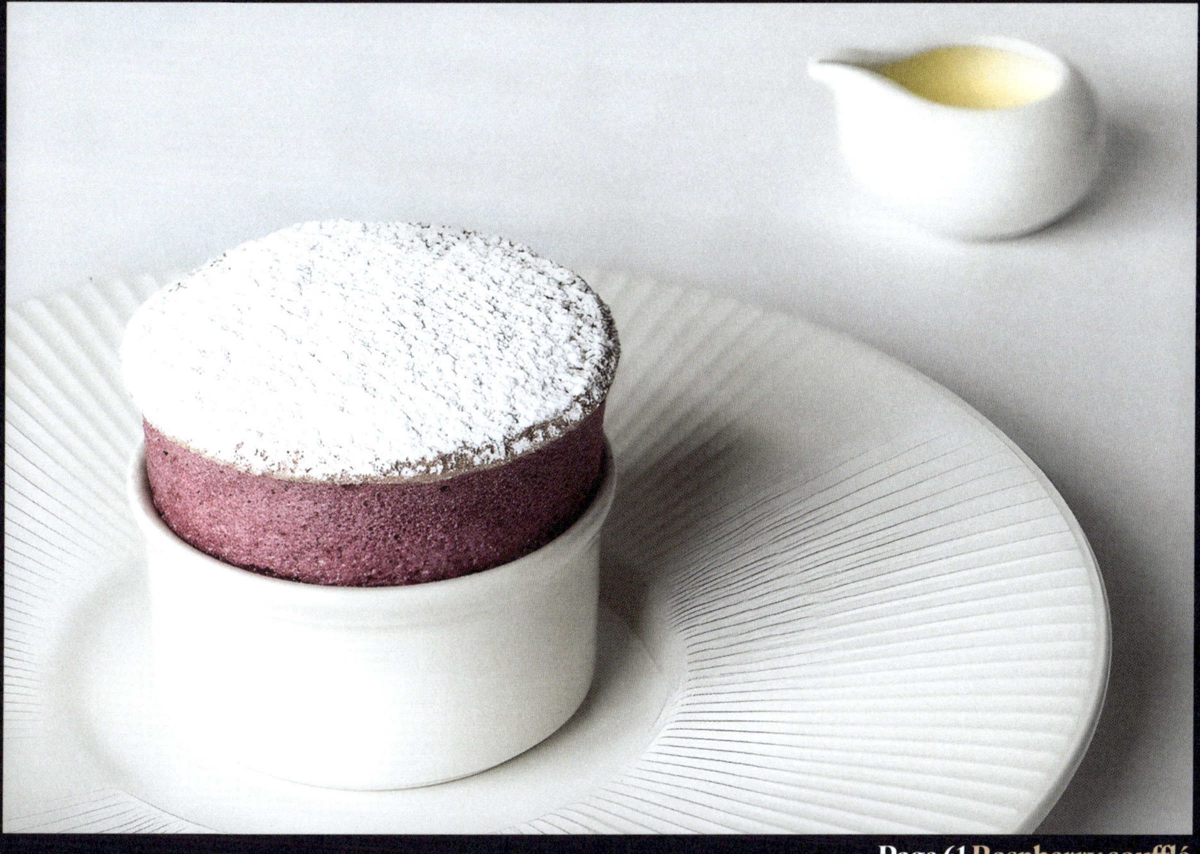

Page 61 Raspberry soufflé

Chicken parfait

Ingredients

Chicken liver - 400g
Whole eggs - 4
Clarified butter - 400g
Salt - 1 tbsp

For the reduction

Thyme - 3g
Rosemary - 3g
Garlice - 3g
Bay leaf - 3g
Shallot - 100g
Maderia - 50ml
Port - 50ml
Brandy - 50ml

For the glaze

Armagh apple - 1
Sugar - 200g
Water - 100g
Glucose - 20g
Red apple purée - 300g
Agar - 5g

For the brioche

00 flour - 500g
Water - 225ml
Egg - 1
Butter - 75g
Sugar - 45g
Salt - 10g
Yeast - 25g

For the egg wash

Egg white - 30g
Water - 30g

Method

Serves 6

For the parfait Bring the chicken livers and eggs to room temperature.

In a pot reduce all the reduction ingredients to a syrup. Strain the reduction once cooled and add to the chicken livers and eggs. Slowly add the butter while blitzing. Season to taste. Pour into the moulds and cling film. Place in a ban-marie and cook at 100°C for 45 mins. Remove the cling film and allow it to cool. Once cooled freeze to prepare them for glaze.

For the glaze Peel the apple and dice. Add all the ingredients together in a pot, except the agar and bring to a light simmer. When the pot has reached a simmer, blitz until smooth and add agar. Remove from the heat and allow it to cool. When cooled to below 8°C we can pour it over the frozen parfaits and allow it to set in the fridge.

For the brioche Place all the ingredients in a large mixing bowl. Mix at a low speed for 10 mins. When mixed place into a greased baking tin and coat with the egg wash, cook at 160°C for 8 – 10 mins. When cooked remove from the oven and allow it to cool.

To serve Serve 1 parfait with 2 slices of brioche. To add some more flavour, serve with some Armagh apple butter.

Raspberry soufflé

Ingredients

Raspberry purée - 500g

Caster sugar - 100g

Water - 100g

Soft ball sugar - 200g

Corn flour - 40g

Egg whites - 6

Method

Serves 6

Bring the fruit purée to the boil with the 100g of sugar. Bring the 200g of sugar and water to 110°C. Add into the fruit purée mix. Thicken with corn flour and allow to cool. Whisk egg whites until stiff and fold in soufflé mix. Add mixture to a buttered ramekin and cook for 15 mins at 160°C.

To serve When removing from the oven you will have a few moments before the soufflé drops. When serving you can use a custard or ice-cream of your choice.

07 Finn Lough Hotel
Gillian Beare/ Kristen Reagon
Director owner/head chef

Kristen Reagon, head chef

"Introduce guests to new flavours and combinations that makes the food shine."

Finn Lough hotel sits on a private peninsula along the shores of Loch Erne offering guests the opportunity to come away and feel they are infused into the landscape. Everything at the hotel is imbued with the natural elements around it and Head Chef Kristin Reagon interweaves the food into that setting.

From a young age South African born Kristin had a love of food. Coming home from school she'd watch the food programmes on TV and try to recreate the recipes to her mum's dismay when she found the kitchen full of flower! Her sister encouraged her to enter a local cooking competition, and she was awarded a scholarship to study cooking at college for two years from where she would progress on to the Pot Luck Club in Cape Town, a fast-paced high-end venue which was a great place to learn to be a chef.

After a time in America, Kristin came to Finn Lough in 2021. She recalls how, on the first day, she sat on the balcony and thought it was "so beautiful."

Gillian Beare, the owner of Finn Lough added, "Kristin has brought a range of skills and really added to the hotel with her unique style of food."

For Kristin food should be fun, enjoyable and playful. It should also be flavour led highlighting the excellent produce and quality of the ingredients. Feedback from guests is that the food is both incredible and fun.

Kristin's approach is to take familiar dishes such as chicken, sirloin, hake and combine ingredients that introduce guests to new flavours which makes the food shine, and allows them to appreciate the skill, passion and care that goes into creating it.

Kristin is excellent at sourcing local ingredients which she transforms into centrepieces of a dish and augment them with elements from other cuisines that add a "wow "factor to the flavour. Finn Lough Restaurant has 45 seats and is always busy, especially at weekends. Gillian adds that Finn Lough has "lots of tentacles and we're doing lots of fun stuff."

There's always something going on for guests that the kitchen plays a part in such as home-made cookies being available in guest's rooms on arrival. There's also a choice of cheeseboard, sweet selection or grazing board, all with local, natural ingredients. Bar snacks and breakfast hampers are also available.

Kristin is a strong advocate for females in hospitality to have their voices heard and treated as equals. She comes from a long line of strong females in her family who have greatly inspired her.

For Gillian and Kristin, there's so much incredible produce still to discover in Northern Ireland. It's a great and exciting time to be involved in food and hospitality locally.

Gillian says, "once you're through the gates of the 75-acre private peninsula at Lough Finn, you feel you are transported to another place." Kristin adds, "the food on offer will help transport you to that other place."

Bread to share: sesame crusted ciabatta loaf

Ingredients

Strong bread flour - 4 cups

Sugar - 1/3 cup

Salt - 1 tsp

Instant yeast - 2 tbsp

Olive oil - 1/4 cup

Water - 2 cups. Luke warm

Sesame seeds - 100g. White and black. Toasted.

Maldon sea salt

Method

Serves 4

Preheat oven to 195°C. In a small bowl add sugar, water and yeast. Mix well and set aside for 10 mins, this activates the yeast (if the water is too hot, it will kill the yeast and the bread will not rise).

In a large bowl add flour and salt. Add in the water mixture and mix using your hands until it forms a dough. Lightly dust the flour on a clean kitchen table and place the dough mixture onto the table.

Knead the dough for 10 mins, this activates the gluten in the dough. Dough should bounce back when poked.

Transfer dough into a well oiled, clean bowl and cover with a kitchen towel. Leave in a warm area to rise and double in size.

Once your dough has doubled in size, transfer onto a light dusted clean surface and shape the dough to fit into a loaf tin (your loaf tin needs to be lined with parchment paper).

Once transferred, cover with kitchen towel and allow to double in size in a warm area. Once the dough has doubled – with a pastry brush lightly coat the loaf with an egg using a pastry brush, then coat the top of the loaf with the sesame seeds.

Bake in the oven for 25 – 30 mins

Page 68 Short rib with Guinness glaze and pistachio pesto

Smoked tomato, scallops with a pepper relish

Ingredients

Fresh red pepper relish

Red peppers - 1 whole pepper. Deseeded and thinly sliced

Red onion - 1. Thinly sliced

Sesame oil - 2 tsp

Lime - 1. Zested

Coriander - 2 tsp. Chopped

Maldon salt

Smoked tomato beurre blanc

Dry white wine (such as Sauvignon Blanc) - 1/2 cup

Lime juice - 2 tbsp

Cream - 2 tbsp

Garlic - 1 tsp. Very finely minced

Shallot - 1 tsp. Very finely minced

Tomato - 1. Roasted over a gas burner till dark

Unsalted butter - 120g. Cold

Smoked paprika - 1 pinch

Lemon grass - 1 tsp

salt to taste

Scallops

Sea scallops - 12 large

Salt

Black pepper - Fresh ground

Vegetable oil - 2 tbsp

Lime - 1. Halved. For seasoning

Method

Serves 4

Red pepper relish Add all ingredients into a bowl and mix well. Set aside and allow all flavours to infuse.

Smoked tomato buerre blanc Put the shallots, garlic, roasted tomato, paprika, white wine, lime juice and a pinch of salt into a small pan and bring to the boil until reduced to about 4 tbsp.

Pass the shallots and garlic using a sieve into a bowl saving the liquid. Heat liquid in a saucepan. Add the cream and boil until reduced a little more. Lower the heat and gradually whisk in the butter, a few pieces at a time until the sauce is thick and creamy.
Reheating Note Warm the beurre blanc in a saucepan over low heat. Avoid high temperatures, as this may cause the sauce to separate.

Scallops Pat the scallops with a paper towel. Season one side of the scallops. Heat up a pan on medium heat, add oil to the hot pan.

Add scallops seasoned side down, then while that side cooks, season the other side. Cook, without moving them, until browned, about 2 mins.

Flip the scallops. If any stick to the pan, wait a few more seconds then try again. Brown the other side of the scallops, and add butter and swirl the butter around the scallops. Finish off with some lime juice.

To elevate served to guest with a half a lime, that's been cooked and burnt in a pan. This brings a unique flavour to the dish and also makes it interactive.

Assembly Spread approximately 2 tbsps of pepper relish on a plate to create a base. Arrange the scallops on top of the relish. Just before serving, gently pour the heated beurre blanc over the scallops.

< Smoked tomato, scallops with a pepper relish

Page 69 Chocolate ganache, chocolate cookies with a coffee olive oil

Short rib with Guinness glaze and pistachio pesto

Ingredients

Short rib
Jacobs ladder - 1
Oil - 2l
Star anise
Coriander seeds

Guinness glaze
Soy sauce - 100ml
Guinness - 1 can
Maple syrup - 100ml
Garlic powder - 1 tsp
Onion powder - 1 tsp
Orange - 1. Zest and juice

Pistachio pesto
Pistachios - 60g. Roasted and shelled
Basil - 100g
Mint - 10g
Garlic - 1. Clove
Oil - 80g
Lime juice - 10g

Kataifi
Kataifi - 100g
Oil - 10g

Method

Serves 4

Guinness glaze Add all ingredients to a saucepan and bring to a boil. Allow for the liquid to reduce by half. Add 1 tsp of cornstarch to mixture and whisk until thick.

The short rib Submerge the jacob's ladder in a deep tray. Add the star anise and coriander to the tray. Pour over the oil and cover the entire jacob's ladder.

Put into the oven at 160°C for 4 hrs, until the bones fall out, or you can pull them out with ease and no tension. While the meat is in the oven, start preparing your Guinness glaze and pesto.

Portion into desired cuts. Submerge into glaze and cook in the glaze for 10 mins allowing the glaze to be absorbed into the meat.

Pistachio pesto Add all ingredients to a blender and blend until smooth. Season to taste.

Kataifi Coat the kataifi in oil and bake in the oven for 20 mins at 180°C, until golden brown.

Assembly/plate presentation Add pistachio pesto to the plate. Remove the short rib from the heated glaze and place it on the plate. Garnish the plate with dots of the glaze. Top the short rib with crispy katafi.

Chocolate ganache, chocolate cookies with a coffee olive oil

Ingredients

Coffee olive oil
Coffee beans - 10g
Olive oil - 50ml

Chocolate cookie
Dark chocolate (high%) - 110g
Unsalted butter - 70g
Caster sugar - 85g
Light brown sugar - 40g
Eggs - 1
Plain flour - 65g
Cacao - 1 1/2 tbsp
Baking powder - 1/2 tsp
Salt - 1/4 tsp

Baileys stiff chocolate cremeux
Cream - 440ml
Baileys - 70ml
Dark chocolate - 250g
Sugar - 50g
Egg yolks - 3
Salt - A pinch

Method

Coffee olive oil In a pot heat up olive oil for 2 mins. Add coffee beans and cook for 2 more mins. Allow to cool and strain.

Chocolate cookie Melt butter and chocolate over a double boiler. Whisk eggs and sugar for exactly 5 mins in a mixer/electric whisk. To the whipped eggs add melted butter and chocolate on a low speed. Once fully combined, turn off the mixer.

Add flour, salt and baking powder into the mixing bowl and gently fold in until combined. Using an ice cream scoop – scoop onto a baking tray lined with parchment. Bake for 12 mins at 180°C.

Baileys stiff chocolate cremeux In a medium size pot, heat up the cream and the baileys. In a bowl, mix eggs and sugar until combined. Once the cream is warm add a 1/4 cup of warm cream into the egg mix and mix well. Add the egg mix back into the pot. With a spatula, stir the mixture for 3 mins until the mixture coats the spatula. In a clean bowl, pour hot egg mix over the chocolate. Whisk in the mixture. Add salt and set into a container for the fridge. Allow to cool. Once cool, set in the fridge for 2 hrs.

To assemble Scoop cremeux into a bowl. Pour over the coffee olive oil. Serve with 2 cookies on the side to scoop in.

08

28 at the Hollow
Glen Wheeler
Head chef owner

At fifteen, I started working in a local hotel cleaning tables and interacting with customers. What sparked my interest in cooking was a lecturer at college, Neven Maguire, an esteemed chef and owner of MacNean Restaurant in County Cavan, who gave me the chance to work in the kitchen for a weekend. As soon as I stepped into it, I was hooked. I worked my way up the ranks and became head chef at a very young age.

I wanted to know how other kitchens operated and how to run them efficiently under pressure. MacNean would close for a month every January and I would write to top restaurants across the world asking if I could work for them free for a month.

Quite a few agreed and I would save money and pay my way to them. Among the prestigious restaurants I worked at were Gordon Ramsay's Three Michelin Star restaurant in London, Noma in Copenhagen and Alinea in Chicago. I worked all the hours and was a sponge absorbing everything, gaining great experience and knowledge.

In January 2018 I opened my own restaurant called 28 Darling Street in Enniskillen which won loads of accolades for three years until covid hit. That was hard as most restaurants don't make money in their first year of operation, break even in the second and turn a profit in the third.

Our lease was ending at Darling Street, and I had my eye on the basement of this beautiful building in Enniskillen that was 135 years old. The building was home to an historic pub called Blakes of the Hollow. The basement used to be an old Guinness bottling plant where the barrels were rolled into what is now the restaurant. We named it 28 at the Hollow because we wanted to take our customers with us, so we took the 28 from Darling Street to our new venture at the Hollow.

28 at the Hollow specialises in modern Irish cuisine with French influences serving a casual dinner menu as well as a la carte. We source the best of ingredients locally as much as we can as the meat, fish and vegetables in Ireland are among the best produce in the world.

The restaurant has won awards for both the Best Restaurant and Best Chef in Fermanagh several times. We have another restaurant at the top of the building which we currently use for private events, though our aim is to open it fully with a focus on fine dining tasting menus.

Fermanagh is the equivalent of the English Lake District with lots of wonderful loughs, magnificent landscape and a relaxed feel. There is a great dining scene in Enniskillen. As well as restaurants, there are lots of thriving independent coffee shops, cafes and bakeries. We have the talent in town and the produce on our doorstep, and I'm delighted 28 at the Hollow is part of this fantastic community.

"Specialises in modern Irish cuisine with French influences."

Seared scallops, burnt apple purée and black pudding

Ingredients

For the scallops

Scallops - 12. Shell removed, cleaned and roe off. 3 per person. 4 if small in size

O'Dohertys black pudding - 4 slices. Cut in half (8 pieces)

Green Apple - Cut into matchsticks. 6 – 8 matchsticks per person

Salt

Vegetable oil - 1 tsp

Burnt apple purée

Granny smith apples - 4

Butter - 100g. Plus 1 knob for cooking

Apple cider - 100ml

Demerara sugar - 50g

Salt

Buttered apple

Apple - 1 cored and cut in quarters lengthways

Apple Juice - 200ml

Butter - 100g

Method

Serves 4

Burnt apple purée Peel and chop the Granny Smith apples. Heat a knob of butter in a small pan over a medium heat. Add the sugar and cook the apples until lightly caramelised. Deglaze the pan with the cider and then transfer to a blender and blitz until smooth. Add the remainder of the butter as is blends. Season with sea salt and pass through a fine sieve.

Buttered apple With a vegetable peeler smooth and sculpt each apple quarter to resemble a soap. In a small heavy based sauce pan, add the butter on a medium heat. When the butter is foaming add the apple soaps and gently baste in the saucepan for 2 mins. Then add your apple juice and lightly poach until slightly tender, this will take 8 – 10 mins over a low heat.

To serve Place the 8 pieces of black pudding in a pan and cook until crisp on the edges, keep warm.

Season the scallops with the salt. Heat the oil in a nonstick frying pan. When hot, add the scallops. Cook the scallops for about 1 min. Flip to the other side. Add your butter and cook for another min. The scallops should be golden brown and nicely caramelised. They should be slightly under cooked in the middle. You may need to do this in batches depending on the size of your pan.

Place the purée on the plate, add the buttered apple in the centre of the plate arrange the scallops and black pudding around, and top the scallops with the apple match sticks.

Tip Cut the match sticks just before serving to avoid them browning.

< Seared scallops, burnt apple purée and black pudding

Page 74 Caramelised pork belly, date and apple jam, carrot crisp, pickled raisins

Caramelised pork belly, date and apple jam, carrot crisp, pickled raisins

Ingredients

For the pork belly

Pork belly - 800g. Boned, rolled and tied

Garlic - 2 cloves

Carrots - 2

Leeks - 1

Onion - 1

Thyme - Small bunch

Rosemary - 2 stalks

Ground cinnamon - 2 tbsp

Star anise - 2

Salt

Apple juice - 1l

Demerara sugar - 50g

Orange juice - 100ml

Date and apple jam

Dates - 500g. Dried and pitted

Granny smith apples - 4. Roughly chopped

Red wine - 300ml

Apple juice - 200ml

Ground cloves - 1/2 tsp

Ground cinnamon - 1/2 tsp

Mixed spice - 1/2 tsp

Demerara sugar - 200g

Cassis - 100ml

Port - 100ml

Lemon - 1/2. Juiced

Water

Method

Preheat your oven to 180°C and lightly grease two large baking trays. Low and slow is the key to this tasty pork dish. We normally allow at least 24 hrs from cooking to cooling then slicing and reheating so try work a day ahead.

For the pork belly Roughly chop all vegetables and place onto the base of a large deep tray. Add thyme and rosemary. Place pork belly on top. Add spices and season well then add apple juice and just enough water to make sure the pork is submerged in liquid. Cover the top of the tray with tin foil and place into a preheated oven at 150°C for 4 hrs or until pork belly is tender. Check the cooking every hour making sure the meat isn't drying out and still has plenty of liquid, top with water if needed. Once cooked and tender, allow the pork to cool slightly, and remove from tray. Carefully remove outer layer of fat and string from the pork belly. Place the pork belly onto a large sheet of tin foil and roll as tight as you can tucking in both sides. Allow to cool for at least 4 – 5 hrs or ideally overnight.

Add the Demerara sugar into a heavy based pot and soften over a medium heat then add your orange juice and reduce to a slightly thick caramel. Remove tin foil from the pork belly and slice about 1.5 – 2 cm thick and place onto a tray then cover with the orange caramel. Place in the oven at 180°C to heat through and caramelise. This should take around 6 – 8 mins and is ready to serve.

Date and apple jam In a heavy based pot add the dates, apples, red wine and apple juice. Add all the spices and simmer on a low heat until apples are cooked, and dates have softened. Add the demerara sugar, cassis and port and cook for a further 30 mins on a low heat adding small amounts of water to prevent the mixture from drying out and catching on the pan. Transfer mix into thermo mix or food processor and blend for 5 mins adding lemon juice to add acidity. More water can be added too if you find the mixture is too thick. Once the mixture is at a smooth consistency pass through a sieve and store in the fridge until needed. Best served at room temperature.

Tip This is also delicious served with cheese.

Carrot crisps
Carrots - 2
Salt

Date and apple jam
Salt - A pinch
Sugar - 200g
White wine vinegar - 200ml
Cider vinegar - 200ml
Thyme - 2 sprigs
Cloves
Pink peppercorns - 1 tsp
Bayleaf - 1
Water - 200ml
Golden raisins - 300g

Carrot crisps Pre heat a deep fat fryer to 130°C. Using a vegetable peeler, peel the carrots and discard of peelings. Keep peeling carrots rotating the carrot as you peel to create nice long even ribbons. Alternatively, you can use a Japanese mandolin rather than a peeler. Place carrot ribbons into deep fat fryer and cook until carrots are crisp continuously stirring to cook evenly. Remove carrots from fryer, shake off access oil and season with salt. Allow to cool and place in an airtight container until needed.

Pickled raisins Place all ingredients except golden raisins in a saucepan and bring to the boil and simmer for 5 mins. Allow pickling Liquid to cool slightly then pour over golden raisins. Leave to infuse for at least an hour or preferably overnight. This pickling liquor can be used for lots of different foods such as mushrooms and vegetables and will keep in your fridge for 2 – 3 weeks.

To serve Place the caramelised pork belly on a plate add a spoonful of the date and apple jam, top the pork belly with pickled raisins and carrot crisps, enjoy.

Lough Erne lamb

Ingredients

Braised shoulder

Lamb shoulder - 800g. Boned, rolled and tied

Carrots - 2. Peeled & roughly chopped

Leek - 1. Roughly chopped

Onion - 1. Peeled and roughly chopped

Garlic - 2 cloves. Peeled and roughly chopped

Rosemary - 2 stalks

Cumin seeds - 2 tsp

Red wine - 500ml

Mint sauce - 2 tbsp

Salt

Lamb rump

Lamb rump - 2. 280 – 340g. Squared cut

Olive oil - 200ml

Rosemary - 2 stalks

Garlic - 2 cloves. Peeled and crushed

Aubergine purée

Aubergine - 4. Cut in half lengthways

Garlic - 2 cloves. Peeled and sliced

Thyme - 1 bunch. Chopped

Sunflower oil - 4 tbsp

Butter - 200g. Cut into cubes

Cream - 50ml

Salt

Lamb jus

Red wine - 300ml

Balsamic vinegar - 2 tbsp

Light brown sugar - 3 tsp

Thyme - 2 sticks

Rosemary - 2 sticks

Braising juices or lamb stock - 300ml

Mint sauce - 1 tbsp

Sea salt

Method

Braised shoulder Place all vegetables onto the base of a large deep tray or casserole. Add the rosemary and cumin seeds. Season the lamb well and place on top of the vegetables. Add the red wine, mint sauce and just enough water to make sure the lamb is submerged in liquid. Cover the top of the tray with tin foil and place into a preheated oven at 160°C for 3 hrs or until the lamb is tender and just falling apart. Check the cooking every hr making sure the meat isn't drying out and still has plenty of liquid, top with water if needed.

Once cooked and tender. Allow the lamb to cool slightly, remove from the tray, reserving the juice from the lamb jus. Remove the string and gently trim any excess fat. Place the lamb onto a large sheet of tin foil and roll as tight as you can tucking in both sides. Allow to cool for at least 4 – 5 hrs, or ideally overnight.

Rump lamb Place the olive oil, rosemary, and garlic in an airtight container. Add the lamb and massage in the marinade. Leave for minimum 5 hrs, or ideally overnight. This helps to tenderise the meat. Heat a non-stick ovenproof frying pan and place the lamb rump skin side down and sear until golden brown. Turn the meat over and sear on all sides. Place in a pre-heated oven at 190°C for 10 – 12 mins for a medium cooking point. Remove rump from oven and allow meat to rest for 5 mins before slicing.

Aubergine purée Preheat oven 220°C. Score the aubergine and place sliced garlic into the incisions. Place on a roasting tray sprinkle over the thyme and drizzle sunflower oil. Roast in the oven, cut side up for 15 - 20 mins until the flesh is soft and lightly charred. Place in the thermo mix and blend everything on full speed for 6 mins. Intermittently add the butter cubes. Season to taste. Pass through a fine sieve. Serve warm.

Lamb jus Heat a small pan and pour in the red wine and vinegar. Boil for about 5 mins, until reduced by half. Add the sugar and herbs and reduce again for another 5 mins, stirring occasionally. Add your braising juices or stock and reduce until you have achieved a good sauce consistency. Finish with the mint sauce and season to taste and use as required.

To serve Slice shoulder 2 cm thick and slightly cover with your lamb sauce and heat through in the oven. Heat aubergine purée and swipe onto the plate. Slice rump quite thin allowing 4 thin slices per portion. Once the shoulder is heated, place onto centre of the plate, and place rump to the side of the shoulder. Pour more of the lamb sauce over the shoulder and serve. We garnish the lamb dish with some local asparagus and wild garlic.

Peanut parfait

Ingredients

Peanut parfait – makes 8 – 10

Caster sugar - 50g

Water - 50ml

Egg yolks - 3

Cream - 250ml

Vanilla pod - 1/2. Seeds removed

Crunchy peanut butter - 4 tbsp

Caramel sauce

Caster Sugar - 300g

Water - 150ml

Butter - 80g

Cream - 250ml

Vanilla pod - 1/2. Seeds removed

Apple crisps

Caster sugar - 100g

Water - 100ml

Star anise - 1

Cloves - 3

Cinnamon stick - 1

Lemon - 1/2. Zest

Granny Smith apple - 1

Method

Serves 4

Peanut parfait Place the sugar and water in a heavy based pan and bring to the boil. Continue to boil without stirring until the mixture has reached 114°C. Meanwhile whisk your egg yolks with an electric mixer until they become thick and pale. When the sugar has reached temperature gently add the hot sugar to the still whisking eggs, continue to whisk until the bowl feels cold.

In a separate large bowl whisk the cream and vanilla seeds until it reaches soft peaks. To the whipped cream gently add your peanut butter with a spatula. Then gently fold the whisked eggs/sugar mixture into the peanut butter cream until combined. Be careful not to over mix, you should have a light airy mixture.

In the restaurant we use a sphere silicone mould, however you could use a loaf tin lined with cling film. Place in the freezer for a minimum 6 hrs or preferably overnight.

Caramel sauce In a heavy based saucepan, add the sugar and water and bring to the boil, and cook for about 10 mins until golden brown in colour and reduced. Add in the cream, butter and vanilla seeds. Stir over a low heat until you have a thick sauce. Allow to cool slightly before serving.

Apple crisps Make a stock syrup by adding the sugar, water, spices and lemon into a small saucepan, gently heat. Remove from heat and allow to cool.

Using a Japanese mandolin, thinly slice the apples, dip in the stock syrup and place on parchment lined baking tray. Place in an oven at 130°C for 50 – 60 mins or until they crisp.

Tip To test they are crisp remove one from the tray and leave on cold surface, as it cools it will become brittle and crisp.

To serve Remove peanut parfait from mould and place in the centre of a bowl, drizzle over the warm caramel sauce and serve with the apple crisps.

09

No 14 at the Georgian House
Jim Mulholland
Manager proprietor

"Contemporary Irish cuisine with an emphasis on local produce."

No 14 at The Georgian House, is situated within a beautiful 17th century building on the stunning Ards Peninsula serving the finest modern Irish food with a French influence.

My career began when I was 16 and I worked in restaurants in Guernsey for seven years where I learned to cook classic French dishes. Back in Ireland I worked as a head chef in several distinguished restaurants including the Ballyrobin Country Lodge Hotel and Jean Christophe Novelli's eponymous restaurant in Belfast before coming to No 14 at The Georgian House in 2019.

I soon as I walked into it, I fell in love with No 14 at The Georgian House, and it fell in love with me. The Ards Peninsula is famed as a food haven especially for its wonderful potatoes and organic vegetables. We offer contemporary Irish cuisine with a classic French flourish such as bouillabaisse or vichyssoise fused with Irish ingredients.

One of our highlights is salmon ceviche with the salmon cured in poitin from a local distillery called Killowan and served with brown bread. We make our own fresh bread, and all our dishes are seasonal. Our food is best summarised as contemporary Irish cuisine with an emphasis on local produce.

At No 14 at The Georgian House, we repackage and recycle everything, and as almost all our produce is local, our carbon footprint is substantially reduced. We strive to put money back into the same environment we're benefitting from. For example, our egg farmer doesn't just arrive with eggs, but also with garlic, potatoes, rhubarb and wild strawberries from his farm which is a co-operative. Our honey comes from local hives and the jars used to collect it are returned to be rinsed and reused.

We have a great relationship with all our suppliers and know all our farmers by name. Indeed, local suppliers dine here with their families and consume their own meat and vegetables which is amazing!

No 14 at The Georgian House has won numerous awards including Best Contemporary Irish Cuisine Restaurant in County Down 2025 and Best Sustainable Practices Restaurant in Ulster and Down 2024 from the Restaurant Association of Ireland. We also won Neighbourhood Restaurant of the Year in Ireland Casual Dining Award in the prestigious Georgina Campbell guide in 2024.

The restaurant is split into two areas. There is a coffee shop serving scones and light dishes while the restaurant, which serves breakfast, lunch, dinner and a seven-course tasting menu, seats 28 people. We also have a private dining room which can host events upstairs including chef tastings, wine tastings, christenings and wedding receptions. There is a lovely open courtyard and walled garden in the extensive grounds where events and markets celebrating local products are held.

We have a magnificent diversity of culture in Northern Ireland. People have come with new ideas about flavours, cuisines and textures. No 14 at The Georgian House is part of a network called Taste of Ards and North Down which brings together local restaurants and suppliers to provide support to each other.

I'm delighted that No 14 at The Georgian House is making such a valuable contribution to the thriving dining scene in the area.

Vichyssoise, Lough Neagh smoked eel, Braeburn apple, crumpet, smoked gubeen butter

Ingredients

Vichyssoise

Unsalted butter - 50g

Leeks - 400g. Washed and finely sliced

Elland potatoes - 300g. Peeled, quartered and finely sliced

Vegetable stock - 600ml

Bay leaf - 1

Creme fraiche - 100g

Whole milk - 50g

Lemon, - 1. Juiced

Chives - 1/2 bunch. Finely chopped

Salt and pepper - To season

Wild garlic oil - To drizzle

For the eel

Smoked Lough Neagh eel - 50g. Diced

Braeburn apple - 50g. Diced

Crumpet

Plain flour - 150g

Warm water - 200ml

Salt - 1/2 tsp

White sugar - 1/2 tsp

Baking powder - 1 tsp

Yeast mixture

Yeast - 1 tsp. Instant/rapid rise or dry active yeast

Warm water - 1 tbsp

Garnish

Apple flowers

Method

Serves 4

Vichyssoise Slowly cook the leeks in the butter with a pinch of salt over a medium heat until soft. Then add the potatoes and cook for a few more mins, stirring to avoid any colour on the vegetables. Add the stock and bay leaf and cook at a very gentle simmer for 25 mins.

Fish out and discard the bay leaf, then blend the soup until very smooth. Stir in the crème fraîche and milk – you may not need all the milk but you don't want the soup to be too thick as it will thicken further once cooled. You're looking for a double cream consistency.

Taste and season the soup with lemon juice, salt and pepper then transfer to a jug and refrigerate. Serve with a drizzle of wild garlic oil and a sprinkling of chives.

Crumpet batter Place flour, water and salt in a bowl and whisk for 2 mins.

Yeast mixture Dissolve yeast into 1 tbsp warm water in a small bowl. Add Yeast Mixture, sugar and baking powder into bowl, then whisk for 30 secs.

Cover with cling wrap or plate, then place in a very warm place for 15 – 30 mins until the surface gets nice and foamy. It will only increase in volume by 10 – 15%.

Cooking crumpets Grease 2 – 3 rings with butter, approx 9 cm wide, though any ring or metal shaper will do. **Tip** Non stick rings - brush with melted butter. Everything else - smear with butter. Brush non stick skillet lightly with melted butter then place rings in the skillet. Turn stove on medium high and bring to heat. Pour 1/4 cup of batter into the rings (65ml), about 1cm deep (will rise by 60%).

Cook for 1 1/2 mins – bubbles should start appearing on the surface Turn heat down to medium. Cook for 1 min – some bubbles should pop around the edges. Turn heat down to medium low. Remove the rings (you might need to run a knife around to loosen). Then flip and cook on the other side for 20 – 30 secs for a blush of colour. Transfer to write rack (golden side down) and fully cool.

Smoked Gubbeen butter

Slightly melt the Gubbeen cheese, then whisk in soft butter, season accordingly and set into preferred mould.

To serve Place soup in a serving dish, garnish with the diced eel, apple and apple flowers. Serve with the crumpet and smoked Gubbeen butter.

< Vichyssoise, Lough Neagh smoked eel, Braeburn apple, crumpet, smoked gubeen butter

Page 86 Murley mountain lamb cutlets, sauce ravigotte, celeriac, asparagus, courgette

Kilkeel scallop, lobster bouillabaisse, Ballywalter leeks, Goatsbridge trout roe, shell tuille

Ingredients

Tuille

Egg white - 90g

Flour - 75g

Butter - 15g. Softened

Salt - 1 pinch

Red food colouring - 1 drop

Bouillabaisse

Olive oil - 100ml

Fennel - 1 bulb. Roughly chopped

Red peppers - 2. Roughly chopped

Sea salt - 10g

Tarragon - 20g

Black pepper - 4g. Crushed

Lobster shell - 500g

Plum tomatoes - 500g. Roughly chopped

Tomato paste - 30g

Saffron - 2 pinches

Lemons - 2. Juiced

Butter - 40g

Salt

Black pepper

Goatsbridge trout roe - 20g

Ballywalter leek - 100g

Kilkeel scallop - 1. Roe off

Salt and pepper

Butter - 50g

Marrigold Flowers - To garnish

Method

Serves 4

Tuille Mix egg white with softened butter, sieve in flour, whisk together and add a pinch of salt to create a smooth paste. Smooth the mixture into a shaped mould, cook for 7 mins at 180°C. Turn out and set aside.

Scallop In a medium pan, sear the scallop for 2 – 3 mins, turning when seared on one side, lift off the heat and add some butter to the pan, coat the scallop in the frothed butter for 1 – 2 mins, remove from the pan and set aside.

Leeks Wash and slice your leeks into 1cm circles, quickly sweat off in a medium heat pan with some butter for 1 – 2 mins, turning once and season.

Bouillabaisse To make the broth, place the olive oil in a large pan over a medium heat. Once hot, add the fennel and cook for 3 – 4 mins, without colouring it.

Add the red peppers, sea salt, tarragon and pepper, and cook for another 2 – 3 mins. Add the lobster shells and tomatoes, cover with water to a depth of 2.5cm and bring to a simmer. Skim off any scum that has risen to the surface, then add the tomato paste and saffron and bring back to a simmer. Cook for 1 1/2 hrs until reduced by approximately one third, skimming away any more scum from time to time.

Use a stick blender to blend the mix to a smooth sauce. Pour through a fine sieve, pressing the solids with a ladle to extract all the liquid. Pour through a fine chinois, this time without pressing Add the lemon juice then pour into a blender and add the butter. Blend, check the seasoning and pass again through a fine sieve once more. Chill until needed.

To serve Place the leeks in a serving dish. Place the scallop on top of the leeks. Pour in the bouillabaisse. Garnish with a tuille, trout roe and marigold flowers.

Prune and armagnac frangipane tartlet, milk ice cream, elderflower and candied walnut

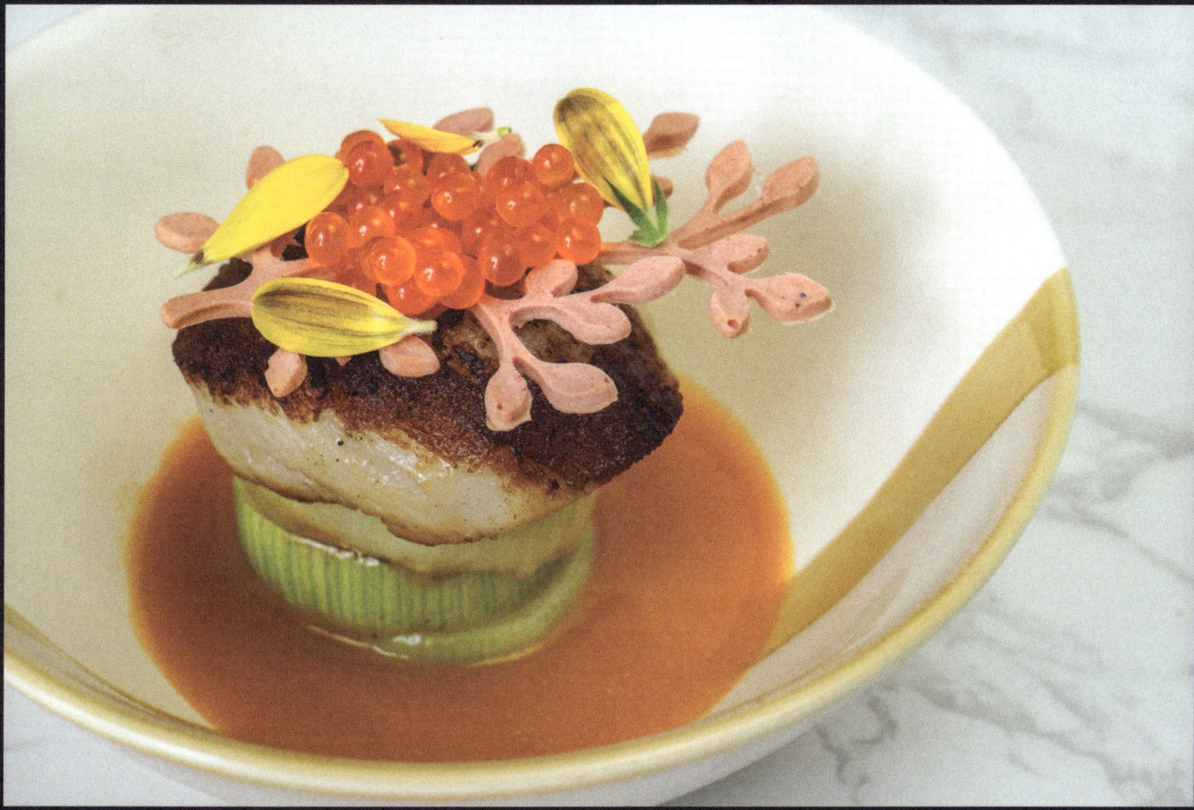

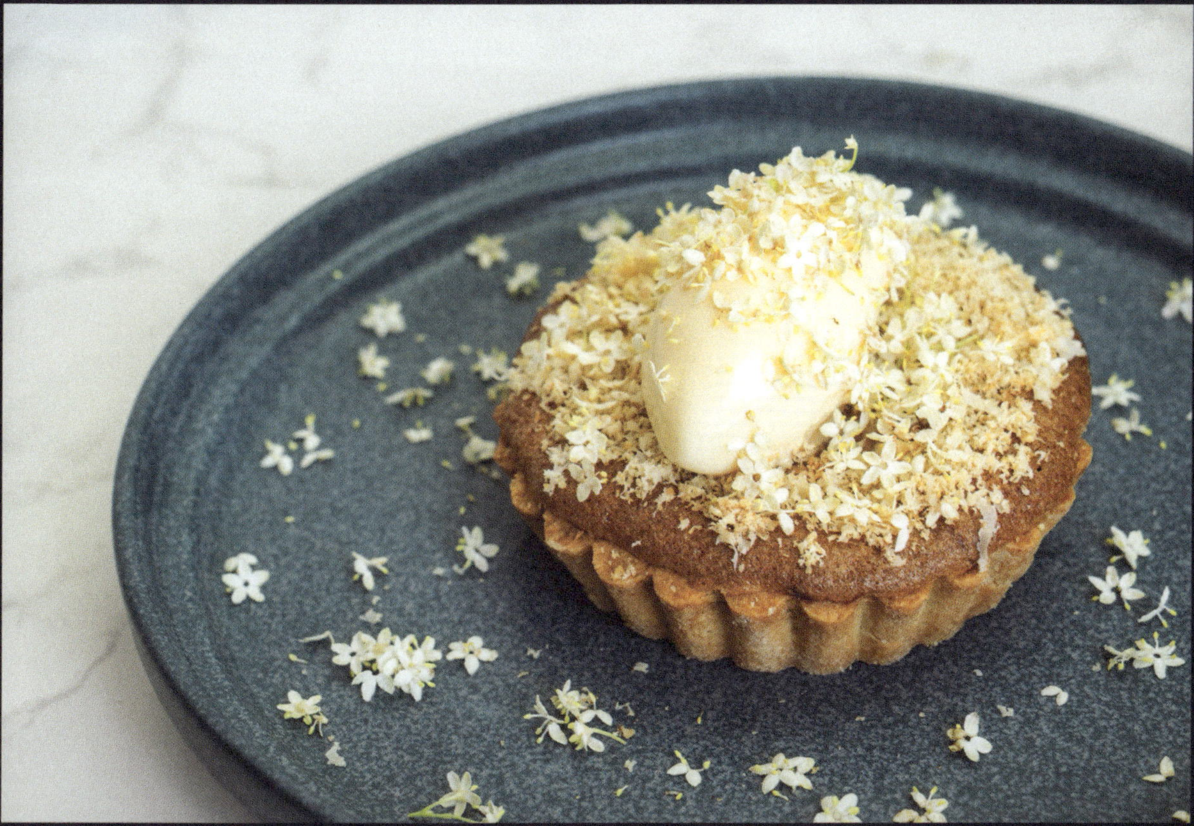

Murley mountain lamb cutlets, sauce ravigotte, celeriac, asparagus, courgette, wild garlic flowers, boulangère potatoes

Ingredients

Lamb rack - 200g. Boned and trimmed
Chopped thyme - 10g
Rock salt - 10g
Olive oil - 20ml

Sauce ravigotte - emulsion

Olive oil - 50ml
White wine vinegar - 50ml
Dijon mustard - 25g
Lemon juice - 10ml
Salt and pepper

Finely chopped

Capers - 30g
Shallots - 30g
Chives - 30g
Chervil - 30g
Tarragon - 30g
Tomato - 30g

Boulangère potatoes

Olive oil - 2 tbsp
Onion - 1. Thinly sliced
Garlic cloves - 2. Thinly sliced
Fresh thyme leaves - 1 tbsp. Finely chopped
Elland potatoes - 300g. Medium sized. Peeled and thinly sliced using a mandolin or sharp knife
Butter - 80g
Chicken stock - 300ml
Gruyère - 50g. Grated
Salt and freshly ground black pepper

Vegetables

Yellow and green courgette - 100g
Wild garlic flowers - 25g

Celeriac purée

Cream - 100ml. Warmed
Salt and pepper
Stabiliser - 5g

Method

Boulangère potatoes Heat the oil in a frying pan over a medium heat. Add the onion, garlic and thyme and season with salt and pepper. Cook for 10 mins, stirring often, until just softened and lightly golden. Place the potatoes in a large bowl and season with salt and pepper. Stir in the onion mixture.

Preheat the oven to 200°C/180°C fan. Take a small slither of the butter and grease a 26cm deep round baking dish. Position the potatoes and onions on their sides in a circle around the outside of the dish, then add more circles inside until you get to the middle– they should be packed in snuggly.

Pour over the stock and dot over the rest of the butter. Cover tightly with kitchen foil and bake for 45 mins or until the potatoes are soft and cooked through.

Turn the oven up to 220°C/200°C fan. Remove the foil and scatter over the cheese. Bake for a further 10 – 15 mins or until the top is golden and crispy.

Sauce ravigotte Make an emulsion with the olive oil, Dijon mustard and white wine vinegar. Whisk together. Add the lemon juice and season. Add the capers, diced shallot, chervil, peeled tomatoes, chives and tarragon. Mix together and set aside.

Lamb Rack Cutlets Marinade the lamb rack in a bag with olive oil, chopped thyme and rock salt. Leave for 1 hr. Take out of the bag and sear in a medium heat pan, fat side down for 4 – 5 mins. Place on a baking tray and cook in an oven for 10 – 12 mins for 180°C. Take out of the oven and rest for 5-10 mins.

Celeriac purée Wrap a small celeriac in tin-foil and roast for 1hr 30 mins at 180°C. Take out of the oven and leave to cool for 10 mins. Remove the skin and dice the flesh into pieces. Add whipped cream to a nutri bullet with the celeriac pieces, purée until smooth. Add a stabiliser and pass through a sieve and season.

Asparagus Cook the asparagus in a medium heat pan for 2 – 4 mins, turning when seared, brush with melted butter and set aside.

Courgette Using a mandoline, cut the courgette into strips. Blanch in salted hot water for 1 – 2 mins. Remove and roll into a smooth spiral shape and brush with butter. Then season.

To serve Arrange the lamb cutlets on a plate with the asparagus, courgette, celeriac purée, dress with sauce ravigotte and 14 wild garlic flowers. Serve with Boulangère potatoes.

Prune and armagnac frangipane tartlet, milk ice cream, elderflower and candied walnut

Ingredients

Prune jam
Sugar - 100g

Water - 100g

Prunes - Juice from 1 small tin

Vanilla extract - A dash

Armagnac - 25ml

Pitted prunes - 1 tin

Pastry
Butter - 79g. Cold cubes

Sugar - 79g

Flour - 203g

Egg - 1 whole

Egg - 1 yolk

Frangipane
Ground almonds - 180g

Butter - 180g. Softened

Sugar - 180g

Eggs - 3

Ice cream
Milk - 600ml

Sugar - 300g

Glucose - 20g

Condensed milk - 100g

Stabiliser - 8g

Egg yolks - 6

Cream - 540ml

Milk powder - 20ml

Candied walnut
Walnuts - 50g. Shelled

Sugar - 25g

Honey - 1 tbsp

To garnish
Elderflower petals

Method

Prune jam Make a stock syrup with the sugar and water. Reduce by half. Add in the juice of the prunes. Add in the Armagnac and a dash of vanilla and prunes. Reduce by half. Take off and set aside.

Pastry Mix the butter, sugar and flour together until it resembles breadcrumbs. Mix in the eggs and mix together to form a fine dough. Leave in the fridge for 30 mins. Take out of the fridge, roll the pastry out to about 1/2 cm thick. Cut out circles to fit your mould. Grease the mould with melted butter. Gently fold in the pastry into the mould. Fill the mould with parchment paper and cooking beans. Cook for 9 mins at 180°C.

Milk Ice cream Mix 600ml of milk with the sugar. Bring to the boil. Hand-blend in the glucose, condensed milk, milk powder and stabiliser. Bring the mix back up to the boil. Add the eggs and cream and cook out to 82°C. Pass through a sieve. Place in a freezer to set. Remix in a packo jet.

Candied walnut Mix the walnuts with sugar and honey. Cook in a hot oven for 4 mins until golden on parchment paper or baking sheet. Leave to cool.

Frangipane Whisk sugar and butter together until they have a creamy texture. Fold in the almonds. Add the eggs and whisk for 4 – 5 mins until combined.

Fill the tartlet with prune jam, add the frangipane mix to the level of the tartlet. Cook in the oven at 180°C for 18 – 20 mins. Remove from the oven and leave to cool.

To serve Garnish the tartlet with grated candied walnut, serve with a quenelle of milk ice cream in the middle of the tartlet and sprinkle with elderflower petals.

10

Tully Mill
John Roche
Chef patron

Tully Mill restaurant situated in the beautiful Fermanagh countryside next to the Irish border, is a destination restaurant offering excellent, wholesome, tasty, locally sourced food. Popular with both tourists and local people alike, Tully Mill is all about modern Irish dining with a twist.

My passion for hospitality has grown from strong family influences. For over 40 years, my parents have successfully run a well-loved local pub, a tradition they proudly continue today. I'm also inspired by my two grandmothers: one a hardworking dairy farmer, and the other a resourceful mother of seven who could turn a single chicken into a feast for twenty.

After training in catering and hospitality at college in Enniskillen for four years, I worked as a chef in restaurants around Fermanagh, gaining experience as Head Chef and General Manager.

Steeped in history, Tully Mill is a restored 18th century corn mill and once formed part of the nearby Florence Court Estate and Gardens. The restaurant is open on Friday and Saturday evenings and Sunday afternoons. Friday is our tapas night where the focus is on casual dining serving Irish small plates Spanish style. On Saturdays we have a set menu which showcases local produce at its best. Sundays we serve traditional Sunday lunches which are incredibly popular.

Our menus are seasonal, using vegetables which are grown in the nearby National Trust owned Florence Court Estate, along with a wide variety of micro herbs and edible flowers. Tully Mill has a long-standing partnership with the National Trust spanning over 13 years.

At Tully Mill we take pride in using local produce and creating new dishes and flavours that are inspired by other local businesses. For instance, our salmon is cured in Boat Yard Gin which is produced locally in Fermanagh. One of our signature dishes is delicious, pan-fried duck with rhubarb sauce and cauliflower puree. We also have an appetizing Irish boxty potato pancake pan-fried in butter or our own beautiful chorizo.

We have a fantastic range of good quality local suppliers. Our lamb comes from a local farm, Mulgarry, while O' Doherty's Fine Meats in nearby Enniskillen supply us with great pork and black bacon. Corleggy Cheese provide us with exquisite artisan cheeses including their distinctive Cavanbert brand.

Tully Mill has won numerous awards including for Best Customer Service. In addition, Tully Mill were delighted to recently win the Best Sustainable Restaurant at the Irish Restaurant Awards. Sustainability is a huge priority for us, the restored water wheel at the mill supplies electricity for part of the restaurant and to minimize waste we even recycle our coffee grinds as compost. This award recognised our commitment to sustainable practices.

With Tully Mill self-catering cottages nearby, we offer a complete experience for tourists, and our prime location in the unique Cuilcagh Lakelands Geopark places Tully Mill at the heart of Ireland's thriving tourist scene.

"We take pride in using local produce and creating new dishes."

Boatyard gin cured salmon, cucumber gel, beetroot puree and raspberry vinaigrette

Ingredients

For cured salmon

One salmon side - 600g. Skinned and pin boned, with belly removed

The cure

Beetroot - 2 Medium. Boiled, peeled, and diced

Oranges - 2. Zested

Juniper berry - 2 tbsp

Boatyard gin - 50ml

Coarse sea salt - 200g

Golden caster sugar - 200g

For cucumber and gin gel

Cucumber - 1/2

Boatyard gin - 50ml

Xanthan gum - 5g

For raspberry vinaigrette

Raspberry vinegar - 50ml

Golden caster sugar - 50g

Ginger - 5cm. Peeled and grated

For beetroot purée

Beetroots - 5 Small. Boiled and peeled

Garlic - 2 Cloves. Chopped

Lime - 1. Juice

Olive oil - 30ml

Sea salt - 1/2 tsp

Mild chilli powder - 1/2 tsp

Ground cumin - 1/2 tsp

To serve

Chicory

Dill

Method

Serves 4

In a food processor, add all ingredients for the cure except juniper berries. Blitz to form a fine paste. Add juniper berries to the fine paste.

Add a layer of cling film into a large baking tray. Spread half of the cure mix across the bottom of the tray placing the salmon side in the center. Spread the remaining cure on top of the salmon.

Wrap the salmon side tightly in cling film and weigh down using another baking tray. Refrigerate the salmon for at least 24 hrs.

Add raspberry vinegar, ginger and sugar to a small saucepan and bring to boil, then simmer for 1 min. Pass the mixture through a sieve, and then chill.

Dice cucumber and combine with gin and xanthan gum, blitz with a hand blender until it forms a smooth texture.

Add all ingredients for puree to a blender and blend until smooth. Rinse well under cold water, pat dry, and slice. Serve with beetroot puree, cucumber and gin gel, and raspberry vinaigrette. Garnish with chicory, dill.

< Boatyard gin cured salmon, cucumber gel, beetroot puree and raspberry vinaigrette

Page 94 Silverhill duck breast with rhubarb purée, cauliflower, baby gem lettuce

O'Doherty's pork belly with bourbon sauce, apple purée, carrot and cumin puree, and black pudding bon bon

Ingredients

For pork belly

Pork belly - 1kg. Boneless and Rindless

Star anise - 2

Ground cumin - 10g

Ground mixed spice - 10g

Bourbon whiskey - 100ml

For bourbon sauce

Bourbon whiskey - 100ml

Tomato ketchup - 60ml

Light soy sauce - 30ml

Clear honey - 30ml

For apple purée

Bramley apple - 250g. Peeled, cored, and chopped

Maple syrup - 25ml

Water - 15ml

Salted butter - 10g

Mixed spice - 5g

Lemon - 1/2. Juice

For black pudding bon bon

Bourbon whiskey - 100ml

Tomato ketchup - 60ml

Light soy sauce - 30ml

Clear honey - 30ml

Method

Serves 4

Place all ingredients for bourbon sauce into a small saucepan and bring to the boil. Allow the mixture to boil for 8 – 10 mins until it has a thick and syrupy consistency. Set aside.

Preheat the oven to 160°C. Put the pork into a roasting tray flesh side down, mix the cumin and mixed spice into the whiskey and rub over top of the pork belly. Place both star anise on top of pork belly. Cover with parchment paper, then seal well with tin foil. Bake for three hours at 160°C or until pork is tender.

Remove pork from the oven and weigh down with something heavy until cooled. Once cooled, slice pork into portion sizes. Coat the pork in bourbon sauce and cook at 160°C for 20 – 25 mins, until sticky and golden.

Add all ingredients for apple puree to a small saucepan and cook over a low to medium heat until the apples are softened. Purée using a hand blender.

Add carrots and sugar to a saucepan and boil until soft. Drain carrots. Add butter and cumin. And blend using a hand blender until smooth.

Split black pudding evenly into four and roll into spheres. Dust spheres in plain flour. Dip into beaten egg, and then roll in panko breadcrumbs. Cook at 180°C in the fryer for 1 – 2 mins until golden.

To serve Place 3 small cubes of Pork on the plate, with 4 small dots of apple sauce neatly around the plate. Place your bon bon in the middle and serve with micro herbs to dress the plate.

< O'Doherty's pork belly with bourbon sauce, apple purée, carrot and cumin purée

Page 95 Butter milk panna cotta with maraschino cherries and black pepper honeycomb

Silverhill duck breast with rhubarb purée, cauliflower, baby gem lettuce

Ingredients

For the duck

Duck breasts - 4. Trimmed and scored

Salt flakes - 2 tsp

Chinese five spice - 3 tsp

For the sauce

Brown sugar - 1 tbsp

Raspberry vinegar - 100ml

Chicken stock - 450ml

Butter - 20g

Cinnamon stick - 1

For the purée

Rhubarb - 6 sticks

Honey - 4 tsp

Grenadine - 1 tbsp

Ginger - 1 tbsp. Minced

For the baby gem

Baby gem lettuce - 2

Fresh red chilli - 1 tsp. Diced

Sesame oil - 30ml

Light Soy Sauce

For the green beans

Green beans - 16

Clove of garlic - 1. Crushed

For the cauliflower

Cauliflower - 500g

Parmasan - 50g. Grated

Garlic clove - 1. Crushed

Butter - 40g

Salt and pepper - to taste

Method

Serves 4

Mix five spice and salt flakes together. Rub mix over duck breasts. Leave to marinade for 30 mins at room temperature.

Add brown sugar, raspberry vinegar, and cinnamon stick to a small saucepan. Boil until reduced by half. Add 450ml of good quality chicken stock, and boil again until reduced by half. Remove cinnamon stick and whisk in 20g of butter. Set aside.

Roughly chop the 6 sticks of rhubarb and add to a saucepan with honey, grenadine, and ginger. Cook over a low heat for 6 – 7 mins, stirring often, until rhubarb has softened. Using a hand blender – blend until smooth.

Leaving the stem attached, slice the baby gem lettuce in half lengthways. In a hot wok, add sesame oil and red chilli and cook for 30 secs. Add baby gem lettuce and stir fry for 1 – 2 mins.

In a separate saucepan, blanch green beans and add to stir fried baby gem, along with garlic. Stir Fry for a further minute. Remove from heat.

Split cauliflower into florets and boil until tender. Drain and add to food processor. Add in garlic, parmesan, and butter. Blend until silky smooth. Season to taste with salt and pepper.

To serve Place the cauliflower purée in the centre of the plate. Cut the duck breast in half. Garnish with green beans and baby gem lettuce. Then garnish with rhubarb purée and serve the sauce in a small jug on the side to serve at the table.

Butter milk panna cotta with maraschino cherries and black pepper honeycomb

Ingredients

Double cream - 300ml

Buttermilk - 300ml

Caster sugar - 70g

Gelatine Sheets - 2 1/2. Soaked in cold water

Vanilla Pod - 1

Maraschino Cherries - 3 – 4 for each serving

For the honeycomb

Golden Caster Sugar - 200g

Golden Syrup - 5 tbsp

Bicarbonate of Soda - 2 tsp

Cracked Black Pepper - 1/2 tsp

Butter

Method

Split the vanilla pod and scrape out seeds. Add the seeds, cream and sugar to a saucepan and gently heat until sugar has dissolved. Then remove from heat.

Squeeze to remove excess water from gelatine sheets. Add to cream mixture and stir until dissolved. Add buttermilk and stir. Divide mixture into dariole moulds and chill in fridge at least 6 – 8 hrs or until set.

Grease the inside of a 20cm tin with butter. Add sugar, golden syrup, and pepper to a saucepan and on a gentle heat, stir until sugar has dissolved. Once dissolved, increase heat and stir until you reach 145°C and is a caramel colour. Immediately remove from heat and add bicarbonate of soda. Mix until bicarbonate of soda has been incorporated – the mixture will foam up. Tip into the greased tin immediately. Leave to cool.

Remove panna cottas from mould by dipping it into hot water for 2 – 3 secs. Gently shake mould to release from the sides and turn out onto a plate.

Serve with maraschino cherries and black pepper honeycomb.

11

The Tailor's House
Lauren Madison Shimmin
Head chef

"The food is above your expectations for what you think you'd get from a wee village pub. It's going to blow your mind."

The Tailor's House is a beautiful old village pub with lots of character and charm, lovely guest rooms and a fantastic function room.

My first job as a chef was in a busy restaurant called Papa Joe's in Bangor. Doing 150 covers on a busy night is a great foundation for a chef and I learned so much from the head chef, Debbie Murray who was inspiring. She motivated me to go further, and I became chef at a quiet village pub with only a kitchen porter. Within four years, the restaurant was packed to the rafters every week and folk were praising the well-made, simple but fresh food.

From there I became head chef at Grace Neils, one of Ireland's oldest pubs. During covid, I was working with a pastry chef who'd started a pop-up. On the back of that we decided to open a restaurant, A Peculiar Tea, in Belfast city centre. We had a menu, dishes and props based on different themes such as Harry Potter, Tim Burton and so on. It was magical and we took Belfast by storm.

I started at Tailor's House two years ago. The food is above your expectations for what you think you'd get from a wee village pub. It's going to blow your mind. That's the kind of comment I get from guests all the time.

I love trying new techniques and ways to enhance the dish, such as duck which I'll cure and process to get the most flavour from it. Our most popular dish is Silverhill duck, which I think, is the best in the world, local to the restaurant

We use local suppliers, and we own the local butchers, Quinns, where we get our meat, chicken and deer from. Our ice cream, which is the smoothest ice cream ever, we get from Dungannon just up the road.

We're taking local everyday ingredients and getting the best out of them. At lunchtime we serve a simple brunch menu such as fish and chips or avocado and toast, but as long as it's done well it's going to be enjoyed by everyone. My mentor, Debbie, once said to me, "if you need to think about it, it's not right. If you're thinking, can I get away with this, then it's not right." That's stuck with me all through my career.

There're six staff, including me, in the kitchen. We've doubled in size and significantly Increased business and typically have up to 200 covers on a Saturday. The staff at Tailors House, including the owner Emmett are great, the craic is brilliant, and we are a wee family unit.

Talking of funny stories, there was a guy I once worked with (not at Tailors) who couldn't be bothered washing potatoes and put them in the dishwasher! Yes, I had to sack him.

The Tailors House is in a lovely part of the country. People in Northern Ireland are outgoing and up for a laugh and we're seeing more tourists. Business is doing well and we're confident about the future.

Scallops, cauliflower puree, truffled chicken butter, candied bacon

Ingredients

Scallops

Scallops - 12. Roe removed and cleaned

Cauliflower purée

Cauliflower - 1 head. Leaves removed and roughly chopped

Onion - Finely sliced

Heavy cream - 475ml

Thyme - 1 sprig

Truffled chicken butter

Chicken skin - 250g

Butter salted - 125g. Room temperature

Fresh truffle - 30g

Candied bacon

Bacon lardons - 250g

Dark brown sugar - 100g

Method

Cauliflower purée Start by adding a little oil to a saucepan and place on a medium to high heat and add the onions to sweat down for 2 – 3 mins until soft with little colour. Next add the cauliflower, thyme, salt and pepper. Cook for a further 2 – 3 mins then add the heavy cream. Simmer for 12 – 15 mins or until cauliflower is fully cooked. Add to a jug blender and blend for 2 – 3 mins until completely smooth. Add more salt and pepper to taste. If you need to adjust the consistency, just use some more heavy cream.

Truffled chicken butter Place the chicken skin in a saucepan and cover with cold water. On a high heat, boil skins for 45 – 50 mins or until all that is left is the golden chicken fat. Combine the butter and fat together and mix thoroughly, finish by fine grating in the fresh truffle.

Candied bacon Place lardons on a roasting tray and place in a fan oven at 180°C and roast until crispy for 10 – 12 mins. Remove from oven and carefully drain fat from the lardons. Keep the lardons on the roasting tray and add in sugar, mix and place bacon into the oven for a further 8 – 10 mins until sticky.

To serve Season scallops with salt and pepper and pan fry with a little oil on high heat for 1 – 2 mins on each side. Finish them in the pan with the chicken truffled butter, basting for around 30 secs. Then remove from heat. In 4 warm bowls add in the hot cauliflower purée and 3 scallops per serving. Drizzle with some of the truffled chicken butter. Add in some of the candied bacon and finish with a fresh shaving of truffle.

< Scallops, cauliflower puree, truffled chicken butter, candied bacon

Page 102 Whole plaice, brown shrimp, cucumber and caper sauce

Beef cheek, smoked potato puree, confit king oyster mushrooms, crispy and pickled shallots

Ingredients

Beef cheek

Beef cheek - 2. Remove and excess fat and sinew. Cut in half.
Onion - 1. Roughly chopped
Carrot - 1. Peeled and sliced
Celery - 4 sticks. Washed and sliced
Garlic clove - 6. Remove skin and crush using the side of your knife
Thyme - 8 sprigs
Rosemary - 2 sprigs
Bay leaf - 4
Veal stock - 2l
Tomato paste - 4 tbsp

Smoked potato purée

Potatoes - 4 large. Suitable for mashing. Peeled and quartered.
Heavy cream - 500ml
Butter - 200g. Cubed
Hickory or applewood wood chips

Confit king oyster mushroom

King oyster mushroom - 4. Cut in half lengthwise and scored with the tip off your knife to make a crisscross type of pattern.
Salt - 1 tbsp
Caster sugar - 1 tbsp
Vegetable oil - 750ml

Crispy shallots

Shallots - 2. Peeled and finely sliced
Plain flour - For dusting

Pickled shallots

Shallots - 2. Peeled and finely sliced
White balsamic vinegar - 200ml
Water - 50ml
Caster sugar - 50g
Grenadine syrup - 2 tbsp. Optional

Kale

Kale - 250g. Picked and cleaned
Butter - 25g

Method

Beef cheeks Start by placing a large frying pan on high heat with a tablespoon of cooking oil. Season the beef cheeks evenly with salt and pepper and sear in the pan until all sides are golden. Place in a deep roasting tray with the rest of the ingredients. Mix them gently and cover with tin foil. Then place into a preheated oven at 160°C for 4 – 5 hrs, until the meat is tender. When ready, remove the cheeks from the braising liquid, then pass the liquid through a fine sieve and into a saucepan. Place on medium heat and reduce until you have sauce that will coat the back of the spoon.

Potato puree Place potatoes in a saucepan and top with cold water and a pinch of salt. Boil for 20 mins until potato is cooked. Drain the potatoes and place in a large saucepan. Wrap the saucepan tightly with clingfilm. Using a smoke gun, add in the wood chips. Light carefully, and insert the tube into the bowl, carefully sealing back up the clingfilm and trapping the smoke in the bowl. Leave the potatoes for about 20 mins covered in the saucepan. Next add the rest of the ingredients to the saucepan and simmer on medium heat for a further 20 mins. Transfer to a jug blender and blend until completely smooth. Season with salt and pepper to taste.

Confit oyster mushroom Place the mushrooms in a deep roasting tray and sprinkle over the salt and sugar. Pour in oil and cover tray with tinfoil. Place in a preheated oven at 150°C for 50 mins. Remove from oil and drain on kitchen paper.

Kale Boil the kale in a saucepan of boiling water for 3 – 4 mins. Drain and add the butter. Season with salt and pepper to taste.

Pickled shallots Bring all ingredients to the boil in a saucepan for 2 – 3 mins.

Crispy shallots Combine shallots and flour and add to a preheated fryer at 180°C for 1 – 2 mins until crispy and golden brown.

To serve Add the puree to the plate making a well in the center, place the kale on top of the potato purée followed by the beef cheek and some of the sauce. Add the oyster mushrooms and shallots.

< Beef cheek, smoked potato puree, confit king oyster mushrooms, crispy and pickled shallots

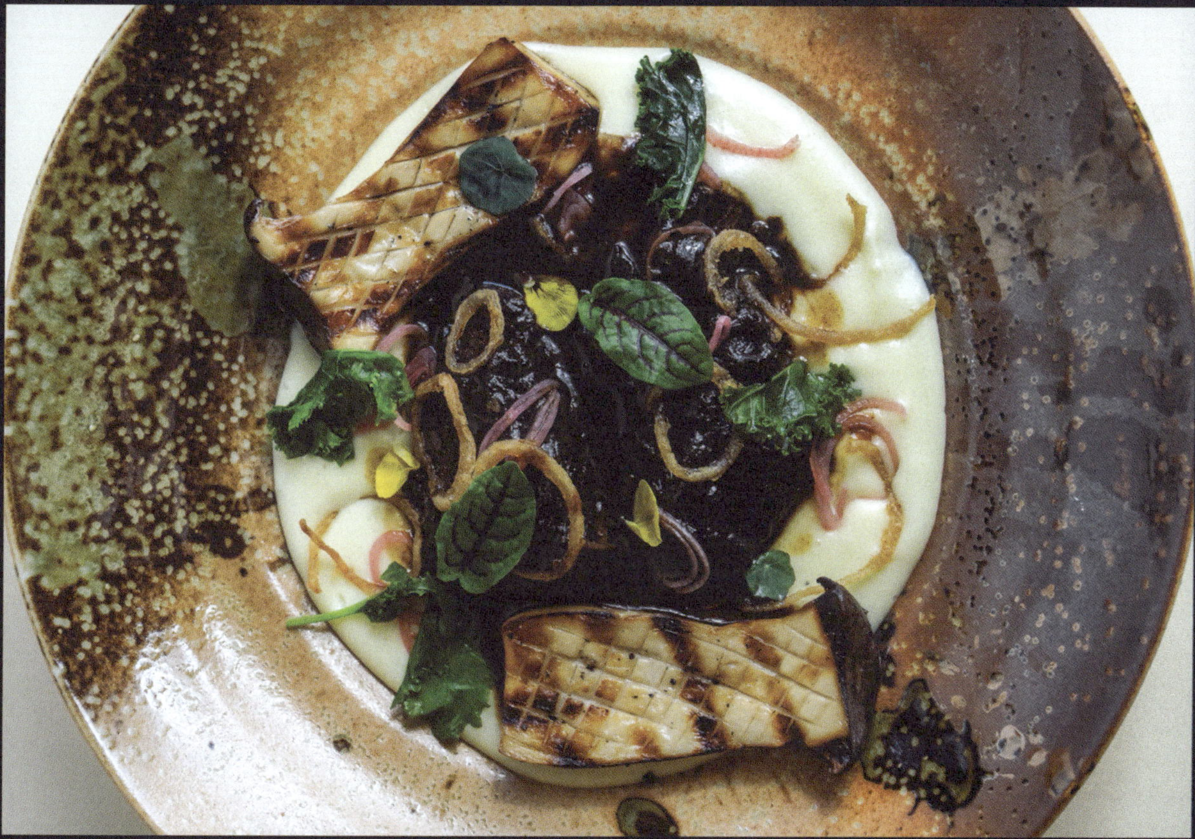

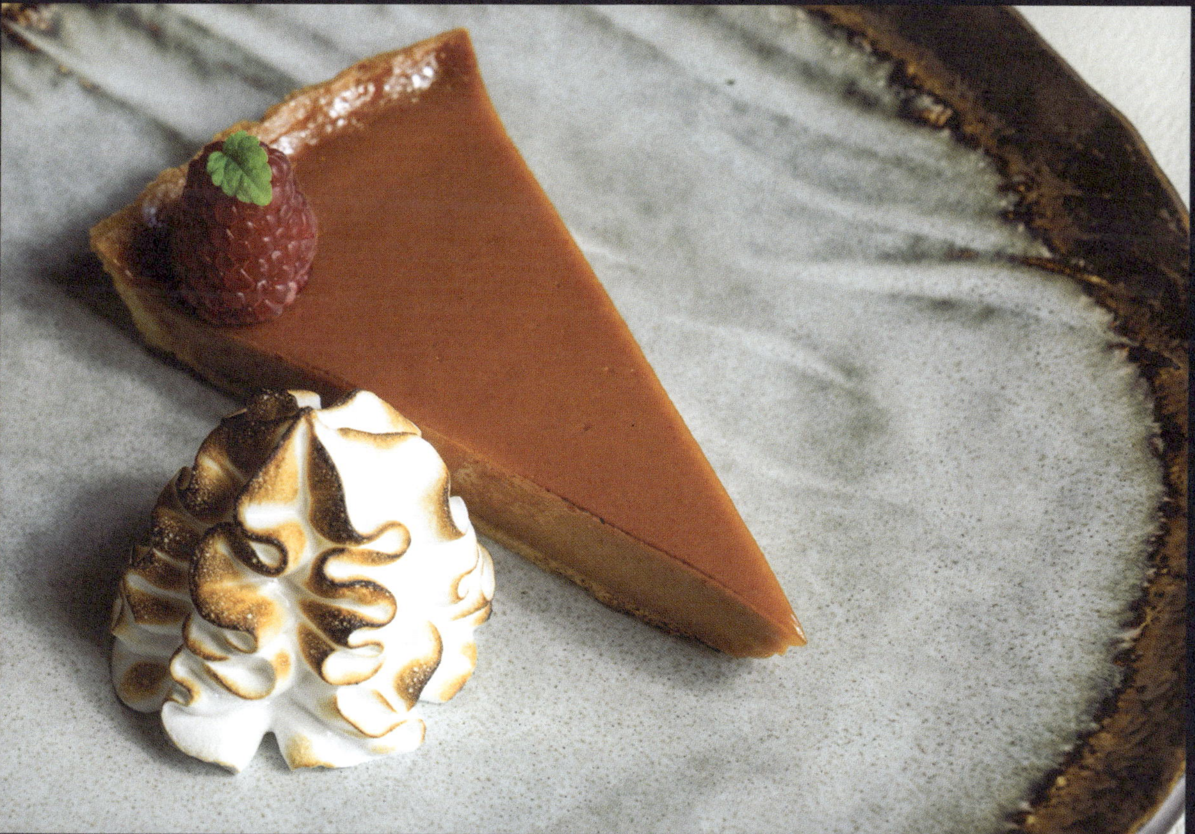

Page 103 Salted caramel tart and torched Italian meringue

Whole plaice, brown shrimp, cucumber and caper sauce

Ingredients

Plaice

Plaice - 4. Left whole, with the skin removed and cleaned

Plain flour - Seasoned. For dusting

Butter - 100g

Brown shrimp, cucumber and caper sauce

Brown shrimp - 100g

Cucumber - Peeled, deseeded and diced into small cubes

Capers - 100g

White wine - 150ml

Heavy cream - 200ml

Butter - 200g. Cubed

Flat leaf parsley - 50g. Finely chopped

Lemon - 1/2

Method

Serves 4

Brown shrimp, cucumber and caper sauce Start by adding the white wine to a medium sized saucepan on medium to high heat and reduce by half. Add in the heavy cream and again reduce by half. Turn the heat down low and add in the cubed butter, one piece at a time, stirring continuously to work the butter into the cream without splitting the sauce. Add in the rest of the ingredients and season with salt and pepper to taste.

Plaice In a large frying pan add 2 tbsp of cooking oil and heat on medium to high until pan is hot. Dust the plaice in the seasoned flour, gently shaking of any excess flour, and place in the frying pan, cooking on each side for 2 – 3 mins, until golden brown. Finish the plaice with some butter in the pan, basting for a further 1 – 2 mins until the plaice is fully cooked through.

To serve Remove the plaice from the pan, let drain on kitchen paper towels and transfer to plate and top with the brown shrimp, cucumber and caper sauce.

Salted caramel tart and torched Italian meringue

Ingredients

Pastry

Plain flour - 250g. Sifted

Icing sugar - 120g

Vanilla pod - 1. Seeds only

Butter - 125g. Cold

Eggs - 1 whole and 1 yolk

Tart filling

Heavy cream - 500ml

Caster sugar - 140g

Egg yolks - 135g

Muscovado sugar - 35g

Salt - to taste

Italian meringue

Caster sugar - 380g

Water - 100ml

Egg white - 150g

Cream of tartar - 1/2 tsp

Method

Serves 4

Pastry Preheat the oven to 180°C, then place the flour, sugar and vanilla in a bowl and grate in the butter. Rub the butter into the flour and sugar until it resembles breadcrumbs. Then add the egg and yolk mix until combined. Leave it to chill in the fridge for 20 mins. Once chilled, roll the pastry until 3mm thick and place into a 28cm tart pan. Line the pastry with baking paper, add some baking beans then blind bake for 15mins until the pastry is cooked through but not coloured. Remove baking beans and brush the pastry with egg wash. Bake for a further 5 mins, or until golden.

Salted caramel filling Warm the double cream over a gentle heat and melt your caster sugar in a separate pan and have the yolks and muscovado sugar mixed together in a separate bowl ready to use. When the sugar in the pan has turned into a golden caramel, very gradually add the warm cream while mixing gently. Once the cream and caramel are combined, gradually pour in the egg and sugar mixture while stirring continuously. Add salt to taste and then pass the mixture through a fine sieve to remove any lumps.

Pour the salted caramel filling into the pre-baked tart case and bake at 100°C until the centre of the tart is no longer liquid but still has a slight wobble.

Check after 30 mins and keep an eye on it – the total baking time could be up to an hour depending on your oven. Let the tart cool to room temperature before slicing.

Italian meringue Place water and sugar in a saucepan, and using a sugar thermometer, bring to 120°C, over medium to high heat. In a stand mixer, using the whisk attachment, whisk the egg whites with the cream of tartare until just starting to foam. Then slowly pour into the egg whites whilst still whisking. Turn the whisk up to full speed and whisk until cooled to room temperature.

To serve Place Italian meringue into a piping bag. Portion the tart. Take a slice for the plate and add your Italian meringue. Toast the meringue with a blow torch and serve with fresh raspberries.

12

The Ebrington Hotel
Leigh Thurston
Head chef

The Ebrington is a four-star hotel and spa in the heart of Derry with two restaurants serving the best of modern Irish food. There's the Two AA Rosette Oak Room Restaurant where we use the finest local ingredients. Or there's the more relaxed Corner House Pub and Restaurant where we serve classic bar food with a twist and elevate it.

My nan instilled in me a love of cooking when I was young. She used to cook great stews and pies. As a teenager I worked in a local pub as a kitchen porter before going on to college and then travelling widely. I worked in hotels in Greece and France then spent nine years in Bermuda where I met my beautiful wife Ciara, a Derry girl. From there I had a stint in New York before going on to the Turks and Caicos Islands before I came to Derry where I worked at both the Beech Hill Country House Hotel and the Corick House Hotel and Spa.

The Ebrington Hotel opened in 2023, where I am fortunate to work with a great team including the formidable Chef Noel McMeel, who is one of Ireland's most well-known chefs.

The Ebrington food offering caters for everyone. If you want fine dining, we have that at the Oak Room Restaurant. But if it's a more relaxed feel and you're just in, say, for a savoury burger, than our Corner House bar will cater for that.

Since it opened the hotel has been a great success with a good name and brand and we're busy every day.

At The Ebrington, we have a real belief in local suppliers and empowering them by using their products. For example, we have lovely lobster tortellini with wild garlic accompanied with a delightful, charred leak and lobster sauce. It's simplicity and elegance combined and not overcomplicating the dish. Our lobsters are sourced locally from just down the road.

Northern Ireland is such a beautiful place to live and to work with such great diversity with the food. We're blessed where we are. For example, all my breakfast ingredients come from within a ten-mile radius; you can't get more local than that. It's real field to fork and the produce here is the best I've ever seen, no two ways about it. It doesn't matter whether it's beef, lamb, seafood or vegetables, Northern Ireland does the best.

In just two years of opening The Ebrington Hotel has been awarded Hotel of the Year from the AA in 2024. In addition, we were awarded two AA rosettes within six months; that's quite an achievement. I can take some credit for that, but there's a great team of talented chefs in my kitchen who have been with me since we opened. A chef is nothing without a team; it takes a dedicated group to make a venue truly successful in dining.

For the first time I will be attending the Balmoral Show in 2025 as a guest of Taste of Ulster representing The Ebrington at the Northern Ireland Food and Drink pavilion which is a great honour for me to continue to showcase the culinary delights the hotel can offer.

"Simplicity and elegance combined and not overcomplicating the dish."

Kilkeel lobster, wild garlic tortellini, leek, trout caviar, lobster sauce

Ingredients

Lobster

Kilkeel lobster - 1

Fennel - 1 bulb. Roughly chopped

White peppercorns - 25g

Bay leaf - 4

White wine vinegar - 250ml

Water - 3l

Lobster filling

Mascarpone - 50g

Spring onion - 20g. Finely sliced

Tarragon - 3g. Shiffonade

Lemon - 1. Zest and juice

Salt-pinch to taste

Trout caviar

Caviar - 3g

Pasta

00 flour - 250g

Egg yolk - 3

Whole egg - 2

Rapeseed oil - A dash

Salt - A pinch

Wild garlic pasta

00 flour - 275g

Egg yolk - 3

Whole egg - 2

Rapeseed oil - A dash

Wild garlic - 50g.Washed. Blanched. Refreshed

Salt - A pinch

Method

Serves 4

Lobster Bring a saucepan to the boil. Add the white wine vinegar, fennel, peppercorns and bay leaf.

Pierce the lobster in the middle of the head with a sharp knife thrusting downwards, this will kill it instantly. Remove head, claws and tail. Cut out the dead man's fingers (Gills) and discard. Roughly chop up the head and legs.

Place the tail in the boiling water for 5 mins and then place into an ice bath. Then do the same with claws for 7 mins.

Peel the lobster and keep the bones for the sauce. Dice up the tail and claws, put into a bowl and add mascarpone, spring onion, tarragon, lemon zest and juice. Season to taste.

Pasta Make a well with the flour, add rapeseed and eggs. Slowly start to work from the inside out to form the dough. Kneed for 10 mins. Wrap in clingfilm and leave to rest.

For the wild garlic pasta dough, wash and blanch wild garlic and refresh. With a tea towel squeeze the excess water from the wild garlic. Mix your egg and wild garlic into a food processor and purée until smooth. Pass through fine sieve and repeat process as above.

Roll both pastas until 1cm thick. Place on top of each other and then cut in half. Cut in half again and then once more, so you will have 8 layers. Wrap and rest for 30 mins.

For the tortellini Roll the pasta to number 2 on a pasta machine and with a 100mm pastry cutter, cut several discs. Place filling in the middle of each pasta dish and brush around disc lightly with water. Fold over to make half-moon shape. Work from the top to the sides to squeeze any remaining air out, then fold in on itself to make the tortellini.

Leek

Leek - 1. Large rondelles, 10cm. Trimmed and washed

Salted butter - 25g

Tarragon - 2 stalks

Salt - 2g

Lobster sauce

Shallots - 4. Peeled and diced

Fennel bulb - 1. Chopped

Celery - 2 sticks. chopped

Garlic - 4 cloves. Sliced

Fresh tomatoes - 2kg.Roughly chopped

Tarragon - 1/4 bunch

Saffron - A pinch

Pernod - 50ml

White wine - 100ml

Fish stock - 500ml

White wine vinegar - A dash

Butter - 50g

Lobster Sauce In a hot pan with rapeseed oil add your lobster shells until they have started to caramelize. Take out of the pan.

Then add shallots, fennel, celery and garlic and cook for 5 mins and then deglaze with Pernod. Add your chopped tomatoes, saffron, tarragon and lobster bones and cook for 10 mins on medium heat.

Add white wine and reduce by half. Add fish stock and simmer for 30 – 45 mins. Blend the mix until chunky, pass through chinois and then reduce sauce by half again. Whisk in butter white wine vinegar and lemon juice to taste. Pass again.

Leek In vacuum pack bag add leek, tarragon, butter and salt. Cook at 80°C steam for 10 mins and refresh in iced cold water.

To serve Cut the leek in half and char in a pan. Cook tortellini for 2 mins. Place trout caviar on leek, place tortellini and add sauce.

Smoked beef cheek, bone marrow crumb, anise carrot, gremolata

Ingredients

Beef cheek

Beef cheek - 4. Prepped
Pomace oil
Carrot - 100g
Celery - 2 sticks
Garlic - 4 cloves. Crushed
Red wine - 300ml
Port - 100ml
Beef stock - 2l
Thyme - 5 sprigs
Bay leaf - 2
Tomato purée - 1 tbsp
Buttrer - 20g

Bone marrow crumb

Bone marrow - 100g
Sourdough breadcrumbs - 150g
Salt - A pinch

Anise carrot

Carrot - 3. Top and tailed. Peeled and chopped
Star anise - 4
Sugar - 100g
Butter - 100g
Salt - 2 tsp
Water - To cover

Gremolata

Tarragon - 20g. Chiffonade
Flat leaf parsley - 30g. Chiffonade
Lemon - 1. Zest and juice
Garlic clove - 1. Fine grated
Caster sugar - 5g
White wine vinegar - 20ml
Olive oil - 125ml
Salt - A pinch

Garnish

Celery leaf
Red amaranth

Method

Serves 4

Beef cheek Light the bbq with applewood. Season your beef cheeks with salt and pepper and smoke for an hour at 120°C In a pan add your pomace oil and caramelize your carrots. Add onions and celery until golden brown. Add garlic, thyme, bay leaf and tomato purée. Cook for 1 min and deglaze with port. Reduce by half and then add red wine. Reduce by half again. Place beef cheek in a casserole dish and add the beef stock. Cover with tin foil and cook at 160°C for 2 1/2 hrs. Once cooked leave in stock to rest for an hour.

Remove beef cheek and place stock in a pan to reduce by half. Make sure you skim your stock every 10 mins. Reduce to a nice glaze consistency. Add butter.

Anise carrot purée Add your carrots to a pan and cover with water. Add sugar, salt, star anise and butter. Bring to a simmer. When cooked, pass the liquid and keep. Transfer the carrots to a blender and blend until smooth. You may need to add just the right amount of your cooking stock back to get correct consistency. Pass through chinois.

Gremolata Add all of your ingredients together and season to taste.

Bone marrow crumb Melt bone marrow in a pan and add your sourdough breadcrumbs. Keep on a low heat and keep mixing until crispy. Once golden brown place on a tray with paper towel.

To serve Make a circle with your carrot puree and place gremolata in the middle. With your beef cheek, place in pan and glaze with your stock in the oven for 10 mins to warm through. Sprinkle with your bone marrow crumb. Place in the middle of the plate and garnish with celery leaf and red amaranth.

Page 106 Kilkeel lobster, wild garlic tortellini, leek, trout caviar, lobster sauce

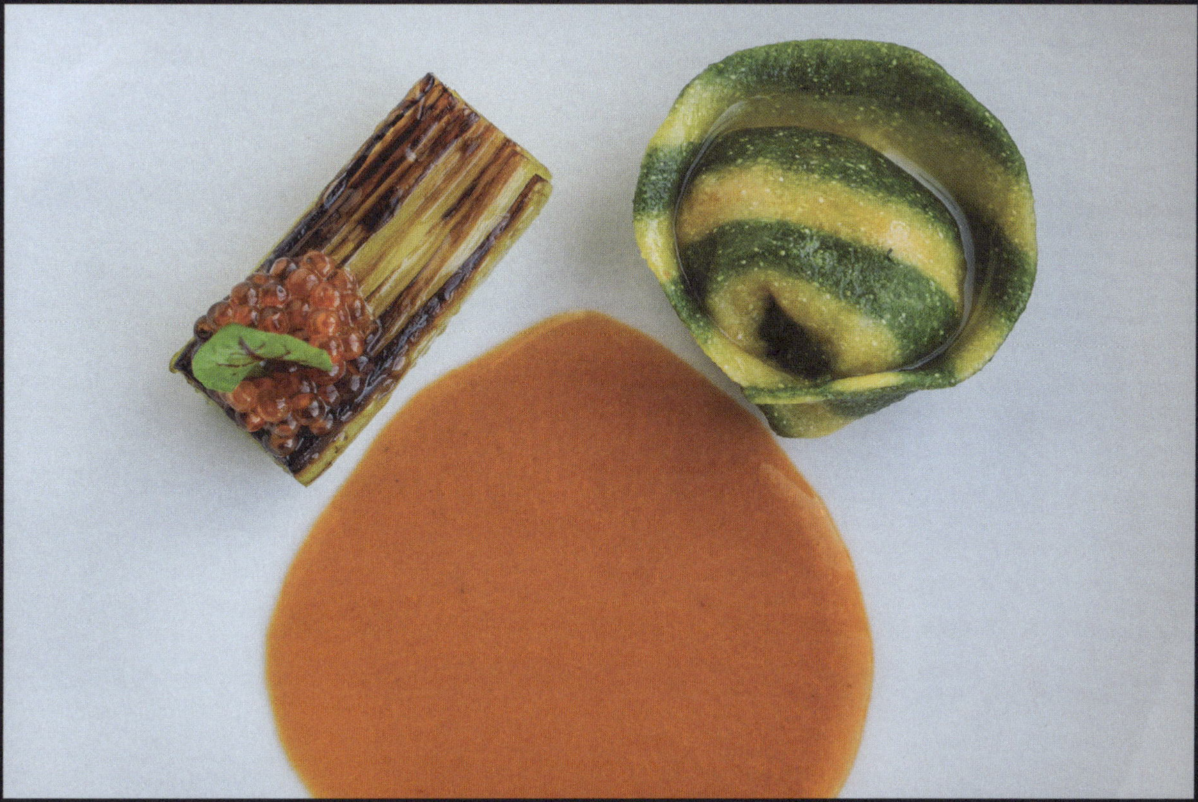

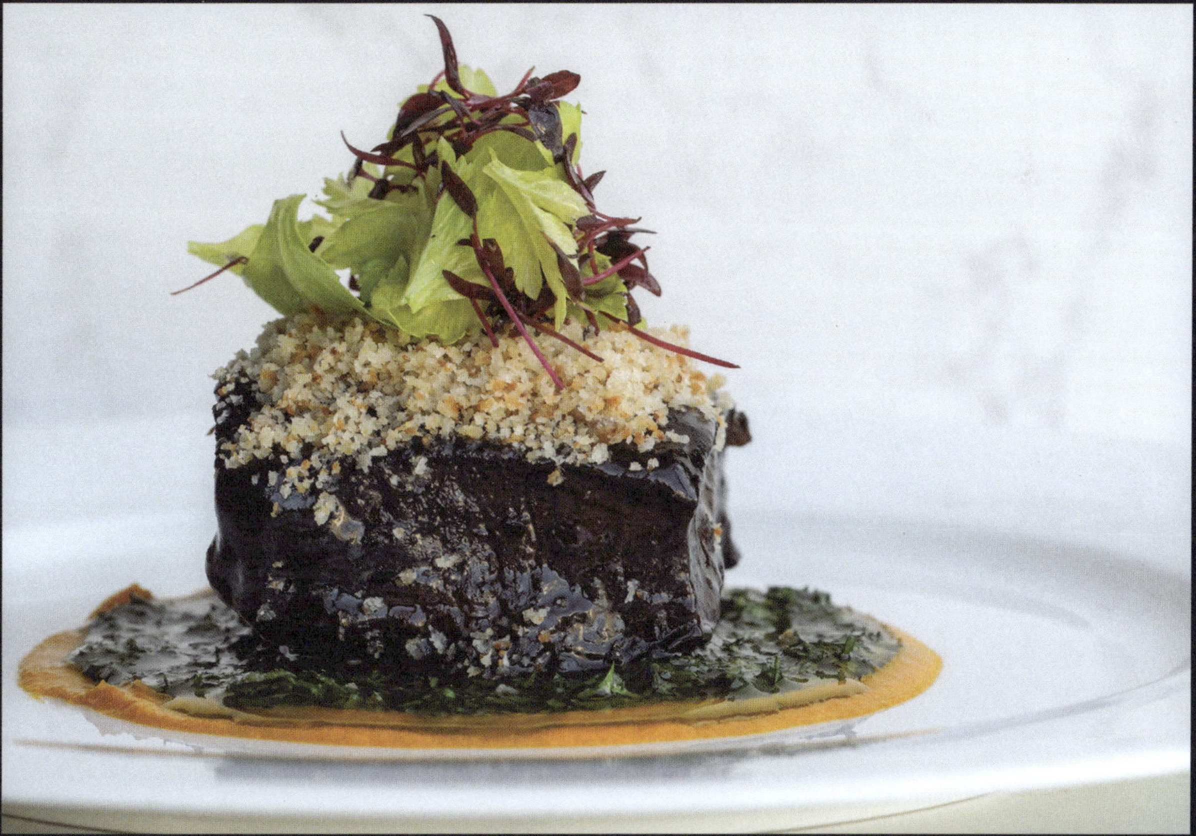

< Smoked beef cheek, bone marrow crumb, anise carrot, gremolata

Mackerel, apple, beetroot, rhubarb, oyster, wood sorrell, fennel, wild garlic

Ingredients

Mackerel

Mackerel fillet - 4. Pin boned

Good quality local gin - Earheart. 50ml

Salt - 50g

Sugar - 50g

Lemon zest - 5g

Lime zest - 5g

Flat leaf parsley - 7g

Dill - 7g

Beetroot

Beetroot - 500g

Sherry vinegar - 50ml

Salt - A pinch

Compressed apple

Apple - 1. Peeled and diced

Lemon - 1. Juiced

Pickled rhubarb

Rhubarb - 4 stalks. Washed

Star anise - 2 pieces

Mustard seeds - 10g

Caster sugar - 40g

Apple cider vinegar - 40g

Water - 40ml

Salt - A pinch

Method

Serves 4

You can ask your fish monger to fillet and gut the fish for you. If you ask nicely, he may even pin bone it for you.

Mackerel Make the cure mix first. Place your salt, sugar, parsley, dill, lemon and lime zest into a food processor and pulse for 30 secs. Place the mackerel on a tray, skin side down and then sprinkle the cure mix over it. Wrap in clingfilm, and place in the fridge for 30 mins. Rinse cure off the mackerel with cold running water and pat dry.

Beetroot Place the beetroot in a tray, add sherry vinegar and sprinkle with salt. Cover with tin foil and bake at 180°C for 45 mins until tender. While still warm, peel beetroot and ball with a parisienne scoop.

Compressed apple Peel and dice the apple to 1cm size. Place into vacuum pack bags with lemon juice and seal.

Wild garlic powder Rinse wild garlic and place it into dehydrator over night until dried. Place in thermomix and blend to a powder.

Pickled rhubarb Wash the rhubarb under cold water and pat dry. Cut the rhubarb into diamonds. For the pickle place you star anise, mustard seeds, caster sugar, white wine vinegar, salt and water into a pan and bring to a simmer. Place rhubarb in pan and cook until tender. Leave it to cool in the pan.

Oysters Schuk the oysters. Please be careful – press down gently on the oyster with a tea towel and gently open the oyster with a shucker. Once opened, place the oyster into a sieve so that you can separate the oyster from the oyster juice. Keep the juice as we will use this for the emulsion.

Tempura oyster

Oysters - 3. Shucked. Keep the juices for emulsion

Cornflour - 50g

Rice flour - 50g

baking powder - 1/2 tsp

Salt - A pinch

Sparkling water - 80ml

Corn flour - Enough to dust oysters

Oyster emulsion

Oyster juice

Pasteurized egg yolk - 15g

White wine vinegar - 5ml

Pomace oil - 300ml

Lemon juice - 5ml

Wild garlic powder

Wild garlic - 50g. Washed

Tempura oyster Mix all the dry ingredients together, slowly add sparkling water a little at a time to make a smooth batter.

Oyster emulsion Blend the yolks, oyster juice and white wine vinegar until smooth. Slowly incorporate the pomace oil. Once emulsified add lemon juice and salt to taste.

To serve Preheat your fryer to 180°C. Place your mackerel on to a tray and blow torch until scorched. Be careful as it will char quickly. Squeeze a little lemon juice on top and season with Maldon salt. Place in the middle of the plate.

With your rhubarb and apple, drain and place onto paper towel.

Place 3 pieces alternate to each other around the mackerel. Do the same with the beetroot. Add dots of your oyster emulsion.

With your oysters, dust in corn flour, cover with batter and deep fry until crispy. Place onto paper towel and season. Dust with wild garlic powder. Garnish with micro fennel and wood sorrel.

Page 110 Mackerel, apple, beetroot, rhubarb, oyster, wood sorrell, fennel, wild garlic

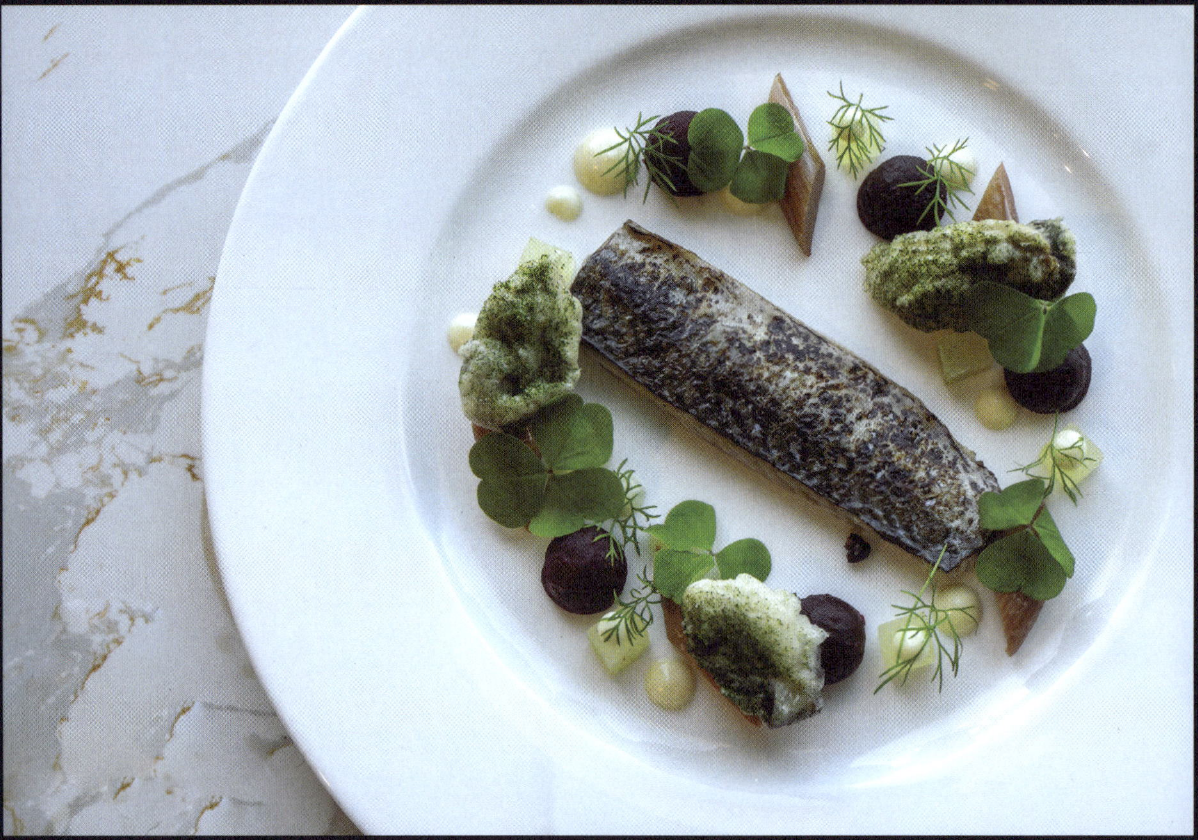

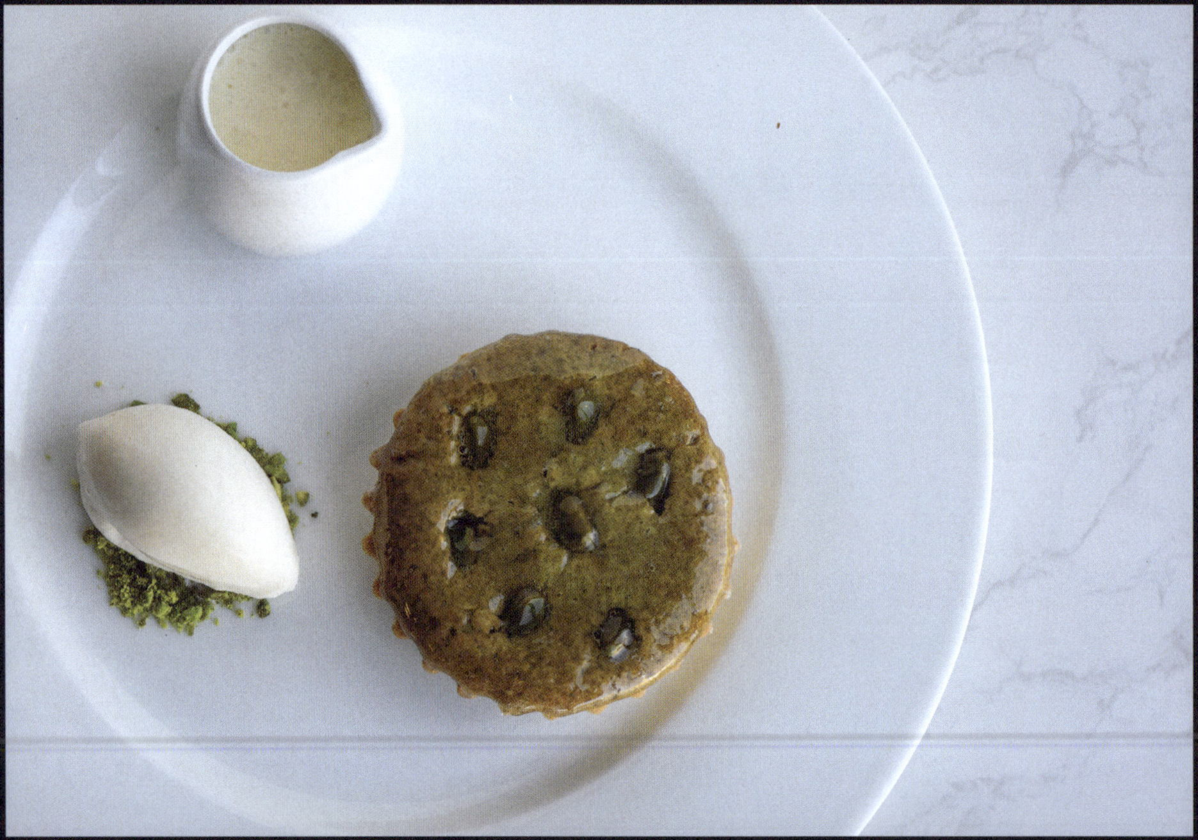

Pistachio tart, raspberry, crème anglaise, yellow man ice cream >

Pistachio tart, raspberry, crème anglaise, yellow man ice cream

Ingredients

Sweet paste

Butter - 250g

Sugar - 180g

Eggs - 2

T45 flour - 500g. Sifted

Salt - 1/4 tsp

Pistachio frangipane

Pistachio nuts - 250g. Fine crumb

Unsalted butter - 150g

Caster sugar - 150g

Eggs - 4

T45 flour - 30g

Raspberry jam

Good quality local producer - We use Doreen Galt

Crème anglaise

Whole milk - 175ml

Double cream - 175ml

Egg yolks - 25g

Caster sugar - 25g

Vanilla pod - 1. Cut in half and deseeded

Yellow man ice cream

Good quality local producer - We use Muine Glas

Method

Serves 4

Sweet pastry Cream together your butter and sugar in kitchen aid. Add eggs 1 at a time. Add flour. Roll into a ball and cover with cling film. Leave to rest in the fridge for 1 hr.

Pistachio frangipane Cream together your sugar and butter. Add pistachio and flour. Add eggs 1 at a time. Place mixture into a piping bag.

Crème anglaise Cream together your sugar and egg yolks. Bring your cream, milk, vanilla pod and seeds up to a simmer. Once your cream mixture has simmered take of the heat and slowly add to your egg mixture continuously whisking. Add back to the pan. On a low heat bring your mixture up to 82°C continually whisking.

For the tarte Preheat oven to 150°C fan. Oil a 10cm removable bottom tart tin. Roll your pastry out to 3mm, line the tin and refrigerate for 30 mins. Make sure there is no excess pastry overlapping the tin.

Add a thin layer of raspberry jam and cover with your frangipane mixture to the top.

Cook for 10 mins and then add 5 pieces of pistachio around the tart and then bake again for 10 mins. Leave to cool for 10 mins.

To serve Place a rocher of yellow man ice cream on top of crushed pistachio. Place tart next to it and a jug of crème anglaise.

13

Edo
Malachy O'Doherty
Head chef

"I believe passionately in good honest cooking with fresh, local ingredients bringing out big flavours. Food should be approachable with nothing over complicated."

Edo is a modern Spanish tapas restaurant in Belfast city centre renowned for its buzzing, dynamic atmosphere. The restaurant serves mainly small plates and we're proud to have been recognised with a Michelin Bibi Gourmand award. At Edo our menu combines modern and traditional dishes that appeals to a wide range of tastes.

I started my culinary adventure in 2010 and haven't looked back since. My love of food developed as a child helping my mum with Sunday dinner. I always wanted to be a chef; I just never had the courage to do it! It wasn't until I was 23 that I took the leap of faith, and through hard work and dedication it got me to where I am today.

At Edo – which is Latin for "I eat" – we've cultivated a relaxed dining experience based on sharing dishes. We serve robust meat and fish dishes. Among our meat dishes are lamb cutlets, confit chicken and tagliatelle and charcoal oven cooked steaks. Fish and seafood dishes include a langoustine ceviche and seafood paella while our range of desserts include delicious churros and apple & miso mille-feuille.

We have a friendly and hard-working team, every day is busy, so it keeps us on our toes. We change the menu with the seasons so we're constantly evolving, providing a fresh and exciting menu.

The owners, Jonny and Charlotte, and I believe passionately in good honest cooking with fresh, local ingredients bringing out big flavours. Food should be approachable with nothing over complicated.

Every day in hospitality is a challenge as it's a high-pressured job. As a head chef you have to keep on top of everyone's section in the kitchen, not just your own! Managing people day to day while keeping your eye on the standard of food is challenging. But with a great team of hospitality professionals around me, combined with having such quality ingredients on our doorstep along with my passion for the industry, makes it easier to produce quality food at an affordable price.

And that's what we deliver every day at Edo.

Scallops, lardo and hazelnut dressing

Ingredients

Scallops

Scallops - 4 medium
Vegetable oil - 1 tbsp
Butter - 100g
Lemon juice - 1/4 of 1 lemon

Hazelnut dressing

Hazelnuts - 200g
Golden raisins - 100g
Sweet cider - 200ml
EVOO - 300ml
Dijon mustard - 1/2 tbsp

Lardo

Thinly sliced lardo - 4 sheets

Method

Scallops Add vegetable oil to a heated pan, then place the scallops foot side down for roughly 2 mins on each side until become golden in colour. Add the butter and lemon to the pan. Baste the scallops until cooked through. Take off heat and allow to rest.

Hazelnut dressing Toast hazelnuts at 180°C for 6 – 8 mins until golden brown. Cook raisins in cider until soft. Combine hazelnuts, olive oil, mustard and raisins. Mix well.

To serve Begin by arranging your 2 scallops on a plate. Place lardo on top of the scallops and allow to melt. To finish, garnish with your hazelnut dressing.

< Scallops, lardo and hazelnut dressing

Page 120 Octopus, chorizo peperonata

Braised pig cheeks and chorizo

Ingredients

For the braised pig cheeks

Pig cheeks - 4
Red wine - 500ml
Tinned chopped tomatoes - 400g
Celery stick - 1
Carrot - 1
White onions - 1
Garlic cloves - 3
Bay leaves - 2
Sprigs of thyme - 3
Sprigs of rosemary - 3

Chorizo dressing

Cooking chorizo - 200g
Dijon mustard - 1 tsp
Chardonnay vinegar - 100ml
Diced shallot - 1

Chorizo foam

Whipping cream - 300ml
Chorizo - 300g
Diced shallot - 1
Smoked paprika - 1 tsp

Method

Serves 4

To braise the pig cheeks Add veg to large pot, cook till golden then add the red wine. Reduce by half and add the tinned tomatoes and pig cheeks. Place in a preheated oven (100°C) for 4 – 5 hrs. Once cooked remove fat off one side of the pig cheek then leave to rest.

Chorizo Dressing Cook first diced shallot in a pan, add chorizo once soft and cooked for 3 – 4 mins or until rendered. Stir in Dijon mustard and vinegar then leave to cool.

Chorizo foam Sweat down second diced shallot in a hot pan on a medium heat. Add your smoked paprika and chorizo, render until soft. Then add in your cream. Bring to a boil and simmer for 5 mins on a low heat. Then blitz with a stick blender until smooth.

To serve Heat pig cheeks in your braising liquor for 5 – 6 mins or until heated through. Add your chorizo dressing to a plate or bowl. Place 2 pig cheeks on top. Blitz chorizo foam until aerated and spoon on top.

Octopus, chorizo peperonata

Ingredients

For the octopus

Octopus tentacles - 4 large

Carrot - 1

Celery stick - 1

White onion - 1

Garlic cloves - 2

Coriander seeds - 1 tbsp

Fennel seeds - 1 tbsp

White wine - 200ml

Water - Enough to cover the octopus

Cured chorizo

Thinly sliced cured chorizo - 500g

Peperonata

Yellow peppers - 2

Red peppers - 2

Shallots - 3

Capers - 1 tbsp

Mint - 1 tbsp (optional)

Chardonnay vinegar - 100ml

Olive oil - 150ml

Method

Serves 4

Octopus Place all ingredients and octopus into a pan of water. Bring to the boil. Reduce heat and allow to simmer until tender (roughly 1 hr). Remove from heat and allow to rest.

Peperonata Slice Peppers and shallots into thin strips. Place into a heated pan with 50ml of olive oil and sweat down until soft. Add capers, chardonnay vinegar and mint (optional). Add salt and pepper to taste. Confit in 100ml of olive oil for roughly 10 – 15 mins.

To serve Render the chorizo in a hot pan, add in the peperonata. Thinly slice the octopus and mix all together. Serve and enjoy.

Mille-feuille

Ingredients

Pastry

Puff pastry sheets - 4

Icing sugar - 100g

Apple miso sorbet

Granny smith apple - 8

Caster sugar - 400g

Water - 300ml

Miso paste - 2 tbsp

Lime juice - 300ml

Caramel ganache

Whipping cream - 1060g. Reserve 260g

Gelatine leaves - 4

White chocolate - 288g

Caramel - 2 tbsp

Method

Pastry Dust pastry with icing sugar and Bake at 170°C for 10 – 12 mins until nice and golden. Bake in between heavy duty trays on grease proof paper. Once cooled, break into your desired shape.

Apple miso sorbet Cook all ingredients, except the miso, together in a pan until soft. Blitz until smooth then add the miso paste. Allow to cool for 1 hr in the fridge, place in ice cream machine and turn for 45 – 60 mins.

Caramel ganache Bloom gelatine in cold water for a couple of mins, then remove and squeeze out the excess water. Boil 260g of cream and add gelatine until completely combined. Cool in the fridge, whisking occasionally until it starts to set. Be careful not to over-whisk as the mixture will split. Whisk remaining cream. Add chocolate and caramel. Whisk slowly until soft peaks form.

To serve Build mille-feuille starting with the pastry. Pipe the caramel ganache onto the cooled pastry. Cover with second sheet of pastry and repeat the process. Finish with a dusting of icing sugar.

14 Culloden Estate and Spa
Mark Begley
Executive head chef

Culloden Estate and Spa is a Five-Star hotel with three restaurants located on the outskirts of Belfast amid beautiful grounds and lovely, secluded gardens. The Estate is easily accessible from both Belfast city centre and the airport.

I started my hospitality journey at Culloden as a kitchen porter and as a modern apprentice. I obtained my NVQS in catering and worked in several great venues including a very busy seafood bar called Daft Eddie's in Killinchy, La Mon hotel where I became head chef, and executive sous chef at the bustling Europa Hotel in Belfast.

After a stint outside hotels, including a time as Head Development Chef for a local butcher, I came back to work at Culloden Estate in 2021 where I was appointed executive head chef. I've always loved the buzz of hotels and was delighted to be back at the venue where I'd began my career. Guests at Culloden can choose among our three dining offerings. With incredible views across the estate's grounds, the Lough Bar offers casual dining to suit all palates. Menu highlights include a distinctive charcuterie with cured meats from the north coast of Ireland or a delicious fried chickenburger using Northern Ireland chicken. Afternoon tea includes cakes, scones and sandwiches made from bread supplied by Irwin's Bakery. We can serve afternoon tea for up to 250 people each week.

The Cultra Bar snuggled in the grounds of the estate, serves breakfasts and an a la carte menu that includes Lisdergan sirloin steak or slow cooked beef, fish or duck confit.

Vespers Restaurant offers innovative fine dining and an eight-course tasting menu. Highlights of the many gastronomic delights include Scallop chowder, with pan fried scallops, confit potatoes and shellfish bisque or aged County Tyrone beef fillet. This is our signature dish that always stays on the menu.

Desserts change often at Vespers but include 'comfort' classics such as crème brulee. We have our own extensive herb garden where we grow rhubarb and serve a delicious rosemary and rhubarb sorbet with vanilla oil and bee pollen. My staff and I love to take a basic dish, such as a custard tart, elevate it and take it to a different level.

At Culloden we're passionate about local produce and supporting local growers across all our restaurants.

My food philosophy is to keep it simple and concentrate on flavour. If you think about something too much, you're going to mess it up. For me there's three key words in cuisine: colour, for how the food looks; texture, to ensure the food's neither too hard or soft; and the taste which ensures the flavour of the dish is maximized. I would say to any budding chef, take your time and make sure you get all three of those right.

Our customers at Culloden are a great mix from all age ranges. People in Northern Ireland are so warm and genuine and it's great to provide them with such great food at Culloden.

"My staff and I love to take a basic dish, such as a custard tart, elevate it and take it to a different level."

Beef tartare

Ingredients

Beef fillet - 250g

Radishes - 2

Nasturtium Leaves - 12

Wet dressing ingredients

Dijon mustard - 1 tsp

Worcestershire sauce - 1 tsp

White truffle oil - A dash

Tabasco sauce - A dash

Egg yolks - 3

Method

Serves 4

Mix all ingredients for wet dressing until all combined. Mince fillet steak and add to wet dressing. Slice radishes into small discs. Pick stems from nasturtium leaves.

Press beef into ring mould. Garnish with radishes, nasturtium and bread wafer.

< Beef tartare

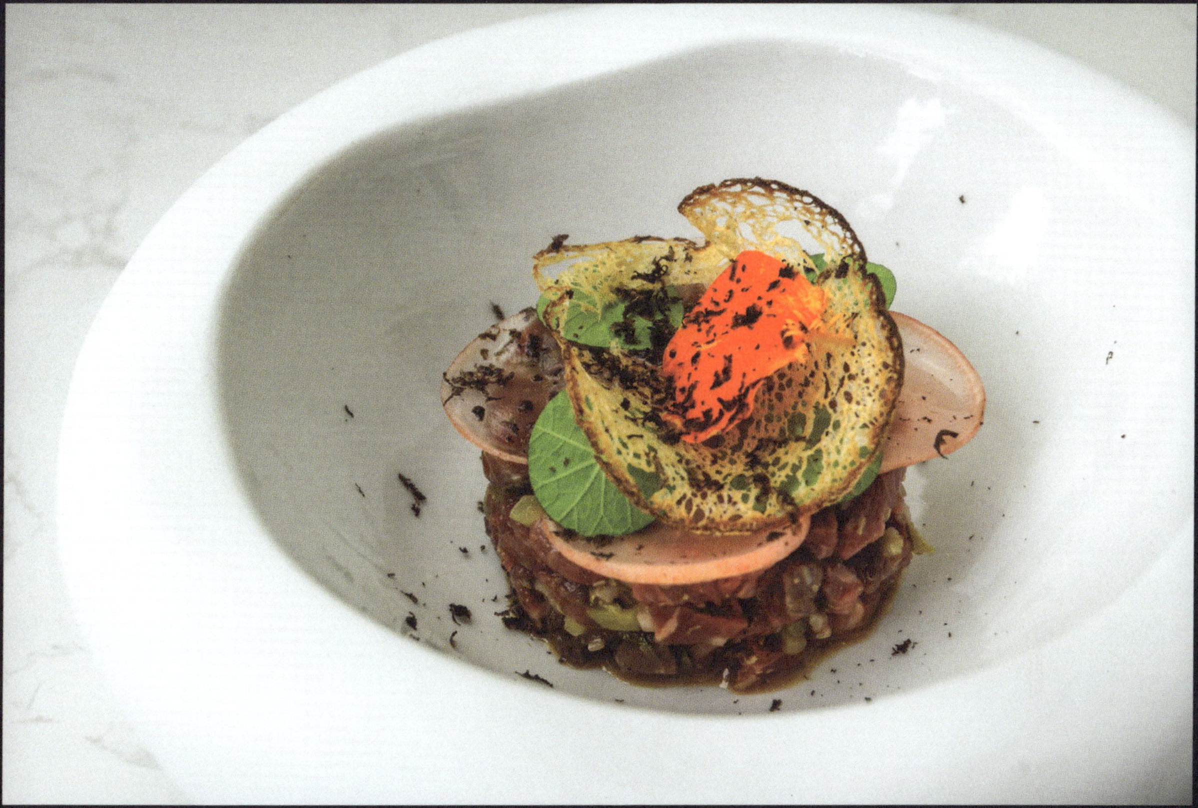

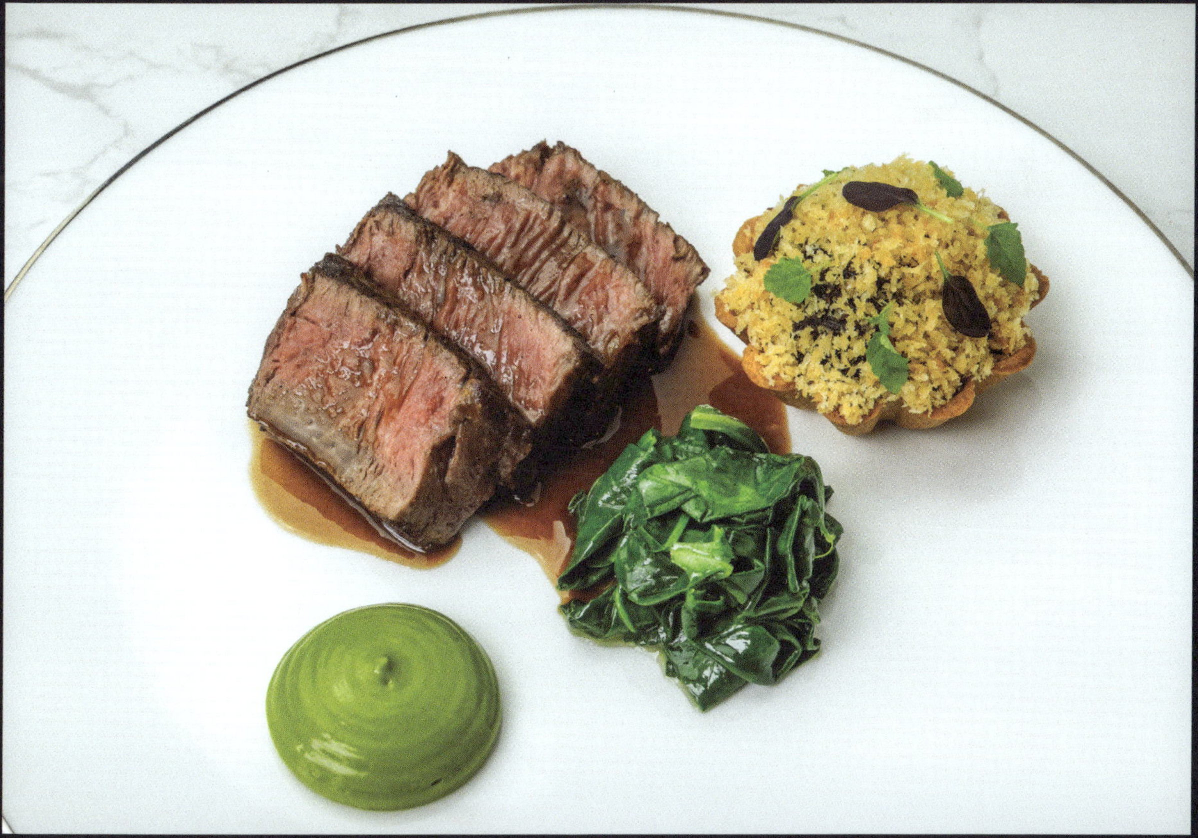

Page 128 Aged fillet steak, ox cheek tartlet, truffled spinach, lovage aioli

Kilkeel crab and scallop chowder

Ingredients

Scallops - 8
White crab meat - 150g
Red chilli - 1/4
Parsley - Chopped
Lemon juice
Olive oil
Salt

Chowder sauce
Onion - 1 small
Carrot - 1
Leek - 1/4. White part only
Celery - 1 stick
Lemon grass stalk - 1/2
Garlic - 1 clove
Soft herb stalks - Parsley, Chervil etc
Black peppercorns - 1
Star anise - 1
Coriander seeds - 4
Tomato purée - 1 tbsp
Brandy - 25ml
White wine - 25ml
Chicken stock - 180ml

Potatoes
Maris piper potato - 1
Butter - 100g
Bay leaf - 1
Peppercorns - 2
Salt - A pinch
Black peppercorns - 3
Star anise - 1
Coriander seeds - 4

Brioche
Bread flour - 50g
Water - 50g
Fresh yeast - 25g

Dough
Bread flour - 450g
Sugar - 70g
Salt - 10g
Whole eggs - 5
Butter - 250g

Method

Serves 4

Crab and scallops Start with cleaning the scallops. Remove roe and skirt leaving clean scallop meat. Lay them on top of dry kitchen paper and dab tops so scallops are nice and dry.

Pick white crab meat ensuring no shells or cartilage are left. Finely dice the red chilli and chop the parsley. Mix with crab meat and add lemon juice. Adjust salt and lemon juice to taste.

Chowder sauce Chop all vegetables. Heat oil in a pan and fry chopped vegetables until browned.

Add lemon grass, herb stalks, peppercorn, star anise and coriander seeds. Then stir in tomato purée and cook for 3 – 4 mins. Add brandy and flambé. When the flame dies down, add the wine and reduce to sticky consistency. Pour in the stock. Bring to simmer and cook for 20 mins. Adjust the seasoning. Finish with butter and lemon juice before serving.

Confit potatoes Dice potatoes to approximately 0.5cm cubes. Melt butter in pan and add aromats and potatoes. Confit potatoes until soft.

Brioche Make preferment, mixing all ingredients together. Cover and let proof in warm place for 30 mins. Once preferment is ready, mix everything together (except the butter) with dough hook for 5 mins. Add butter in several additions and mix until silky and all butter is incorporated. Slow prove the dough in the fridge overnight. For a loaf, tin bake at 180°C for 30 mins.

To serve Finish by assembling the ingredients in a bowl and adding the sauce last.

< Kilkeel crab and scallop chowder

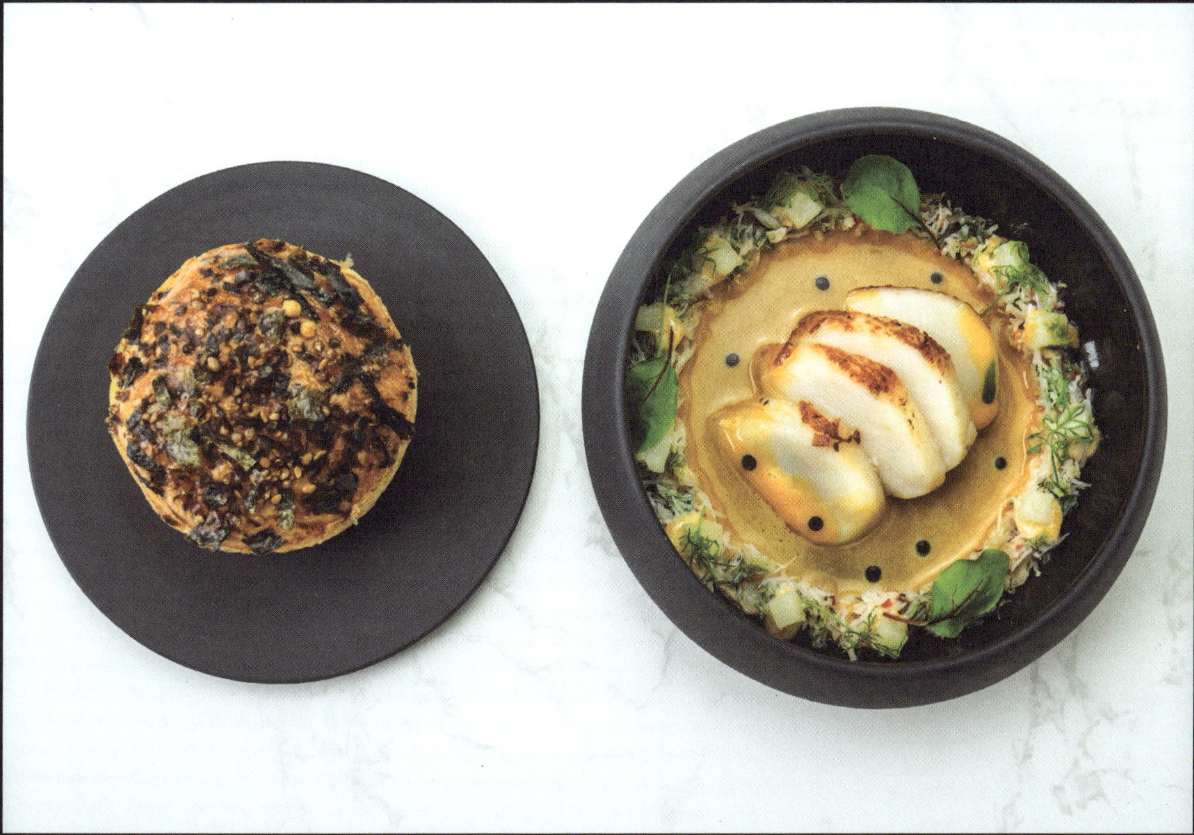

Page 129 Rhubarb and custard tart

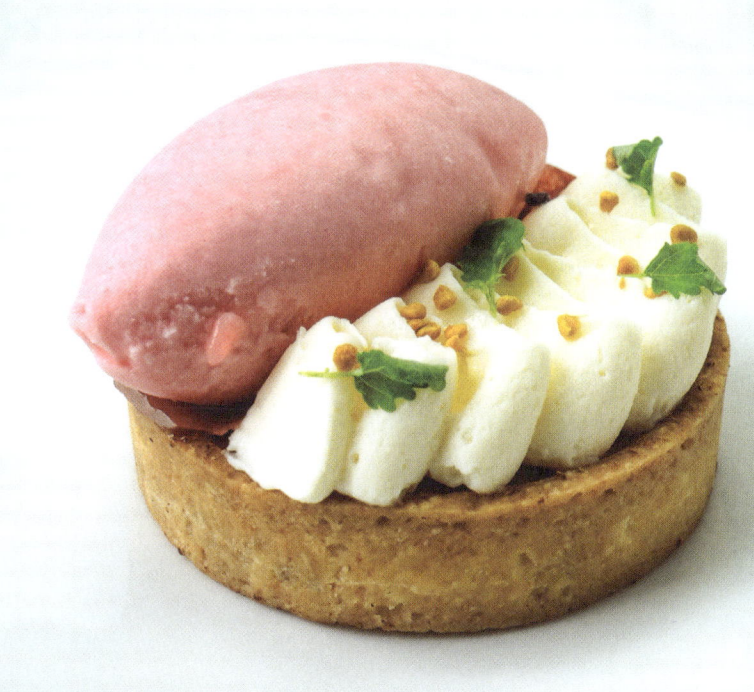

Aged fillet steak, ox cheek tartlet, truffled spinach, lovage aioli

Ingredients

Fillet steak - 4 x 6oz steaks

Spinach - 100g

White Truffle Oil

Shortcrust pastry sheets - 1

Braised ox cheek

Ox cheek - 1

Small onion - 1

Carrot - 1

Garlic - 1 bulb

Leek - 1

Black peppercorns - 10

Fennel seeds - 10g

Bay leaves - 2

Star anise - 1

Red wine - 200ml

Lovage oil

Lovage - 400g

Olive oil - 300g

Lovage emulsion

Egg yolks - 3

Dijon mustard - 1 tsp

Lemon - 1/2. Juice only

Lovage oil - 300g

Method

Serves 4

Trim any excess fat off the ox cheeks. Sear ox cheeks in pot. Add all vegetables and sear until browned. Add aromats. Deglaze with red wine and add water until covered. Put lid on top of the pot and simmer on low heat for 8 hrs or until ox cheek falls apart.

Once ox cheek is ready remove it from stock and shred the meat. Pass stock through muslin cloth or fine sieve and reduce until sauce consistency. Mix ox cheek and sauce together and add around 50g of butter. Adjust the seasoning.

Lovage oil Pick lovage leaves from stalks. Blend it in food processor until all leaves are chopped. Slowly pour in oil to get pesto like consistency. Heat it to 60°C. Once reaches the temperature pass it through the muslin cloth and chill immediately.

Lovage emulsion Mix egg yolks, Dijon mustard, lemon juice together until combined. Slowly pour oil whilst continuously whisking the mixture.

For tart case Line tart mold with shortcrust pastry and bake in the oven at 180°C for 12 mins.

The fillet steak Sear and cook fillet until desired temperature. In separate pan add spinach truffle oil and small cube of butter, cook until soft.

To serve Fill tart case with braised ox cheek. Slice fillet and finish it with flaky sea salt. Place everything on the plate.

Rhubarb and custard tart

Ingredients

Rhubarb and rosemary sorbet

Rhubarb - 800g

Trimoline - 400g

Water - 400g

Rosemary - 6 sprigs

Sablée pastry

Icing sugar - 90g

Plain flour - 230g

Ground almonds - 30g

Unsalted butter - 110g

Whole egg - 50g

Vanilla custard

Egg yolk - 180g

Caster sugar - 75g

Double cream - 500ml

Vanilla pod - 1

Whole nutmeg - 1

Poached rhubarb

Rhubarb - 4 stalks

Caster sugar - 200g

Water - 200g

Grenadine - 20ml

Limes - 2. Zest and juice

Lemon mascarpone cream

Mascarpone - 200g

Icing sugar - 30g

Lemon curd - 50g

Double cream - 50ml

Vanilla oil

Vanilla pod - 1. Scraped

Olive oil - 100ml

Method

Rhubarb and Rosemary Sorbet Add trimoline, water and rosemary to a pan and bring to the boil. Cool and refrigerate overnight, allowing the rosemary to infuse into the syrup. Cut the rhubarb into 1cm pieces and cook over a medium heat until slightly softened, to maintain pink colour. Discard rosemary sprigs from syrup. Transfer rhubarb to a blender and gradually pour in the rosemary syrup, blend until smooth, pass and chill. Churn in an ice cream machine for 1 hr and transfer to freezer.

Sablée pastry Cut the butter into cubes and freeze for 15 mins. Sift the dry ingredients together and rub in the butter. Add the egg and combine. Knead for 1 min until smooth. Roll out to 2mm thickness between two silicone mats and freeze for 15 mins.

Line 8 individual tart rings with the pastry and freeze for 1 hr. Trim excess pastry, bake for 20 mins at 160°C, remove rings and bake for a further 5 mins.

Vanilla custard Scrape seeds from vanilla pod and add to double cream. Reserve scraped pod for vanilla oil. Heat cream to 85°C. Whisk egg yolks and caster sugar together, gradually whisk in warm cream. Pour custard into cooled tart cases and grate nutmeg to cover the top. Bake at 100°C for 15 mins.

Poached rhubarb Slice rhubarb diagonally into 2mm thick slices. Add caster sugar, water, grenadine, lime juice and zest to a pot and bring to the boil. Pour syrup over the rhubarb and cool.

Lemon mascarpone cream Whisk all ingredients together until pipeable consistency is reached.

Vanilla oil Add scraped vanilla pod to olive oil and allow to infuse overnight.

Assembly Pipe lemon mascarpone cream over half of the tart. Top mascarpone with vanilla oil. Arrange poached rhubarb on the other half. Add Rocher of sorbet on top of the poached rhubarb. Garnish with bee pollen and lemon balm.

15

The Street Kitchen
Marty McAdam
Chef owner

"So much more than a restaurant, it's where we create our vision of true hospitality, making our customers feel relaxed and at home"

The Street Kitchen is a unique, relaxed and fun restaurant offering a brunch and lunch menu, and a small plates menu in the evening. It's so much more than a restaurant where we create our vision of true hospitality making our customers feel relaxed and at home.

I started in hospitality on a week's work experience at 13 where I got hooked on the buzz and energy that comes from a kitchen. I knew I wanted to be a chef forever.

After gaining an NVQ and foundation degree in catering, I worked in Michelin starred The Kitchin under chef Tom Kitchin where I learned the fundamentals of cooking. I returned home to work under one of Ireland's leading chefs Neven Maguire in MacNean House where I was promoted to sous chef within eight months. After four years, I travelled through southeast Asia and worked in kitchens in Australia before returning to Europe to become a chef on super yachts sailing to exotic locations worldwide.

I came home and became head chef in a local hotel where I launched my first restaurant: Becketts Dining Room. It was extremely successful and gave me the tools to open my own place.

I found a petite location up an accessible alley in the heart of Enniskillen. It's essentially a kitchen inside a restaurant inside a kitchen. A completely open space with twenty seats, including six seats at the chef's counter.

We have a core team of four, with a few friends who help at weekends when needed and we offer three different styles of food.

Our brunch is very Melbourne style, like our own twists on eggs Benedict and avocado on toast while the lunch dishes are very street food-esq.

Our versions of fish tacos, chicken kababs and bao buns are a massive hit.

In the evenings we offer a small plates menu accompanied by cocktails and handpicked wines, beers and spirits. The lights go down and the crisp whites go on, making it a little more formal but still having that relaxed feel.

We use local suppliers like Lisdergan Butchers who supply our meats. There's a local man who shoots venison for us when in season. Conway Farm bring us wonderful micro herbs and vegetables. All our vegetables are from a local greengrocer, while Albatross, based in Donegal, provides us with our seafood.

The Street Kitchen has won numerous awards since we opened in 2021, including for Best World Cuisine at the Irish Restaurant Awards and fantastic reviews in both local and national newspapers. I've competed twice on Great British Menu which has helped the restaurant gain national fame. We were also recently entered in the Georgina Campbell Ireland food guide.

We've been incredibly busy with a mix of customers from all ages, many of whom have become regulars and almost family to us. The encouragement from the local community has been incredible.

Fermanagh is the Lake District of Northern Ireland with amazing waterways, freshwater lakes and so much to see and do. For a town of only 14,000 people Enniskillen has so many great restaurants and The Street Kitchen has become an integral part of that thriving scene.

Sea trout tartar, cucumber, apple, dill and wasabi ice cream

Ingredients

Sea trout tartar

Sea trout - 600g
Granny Smith apple - 1
Light soy sauce - 10ml
Lime juice - 1 lime
Sesame oil - 15ml
Sesame seeds - 10g
Chopped dill - 20g

Pickled baby cucumber

Baby cucumber - 4
Rice wine vinegar - 150ml
Water - 60ml
Sugar - 15g
Salt - 5g
Green peppercorns - 8
Ginger - 50g. Sliced

Dill oil

Fresh dill - 150g
Vegetable oil - 150ml
Salt - 5g

Wasabi ice cream

Egg yolks - 6
Double cream - 500ml
Milk - 300ml
Suger - 50g
Salt - 5g
Wasabi paste - 25g

Cured egg yolk

Egg yolks - 4
Fine salt - 400g
Caster suger - 50g

Method

Serves 4

Trout Take side of sea trout, take skin off and pin bone. Dice into 0.5cm cubes. **Tip** Chill on a board in freezer for 10 mins to firm and cut easier.

Finely chop dill. Dice apple finely. Add together with sea trout in a bowl and mix well. Add light soy sauce, lime juice, sesame oil and sesame seeds to bowl and mix all ingredients together and let marinade for 10 mins.

Cucumber Slice baby cucumber into fine slices. **Tip** Use a veg slicer or a mandolin to slice. Add all the other ingredients into a pan and bring to boil. Pass through a sieve and let liquid cool. Add cucumber to the pickle and leave for at least 2 hrs (over night preferably).

Dill oil Pick dill off the stalks and add them to a blender with oil and salt, blend until oil hits 82°C. Pass through a sieve and a fine cloth. Don't push the oil through – just let it pass naturally.

Cured egg yolk In a bowl add salt and sugar together and pour half into a small tray. Using a whole egg, make a well in the salt for the egg yolk to sit into. Separate the egg whites and yolks. Sit the egg yolk in the salt. With the other half of the salt and sugar mix cover the egg yolk. Allow 24 hrs to cure and go hard. Once cured wash off and place in an oven for 2 hrs at 70°C and store in an airtight container.

Wasabi ice cream Add milk and cream to a pot and bring to a simmer. Add egg yolks, sugar, salt and wasabi to a bowl and mix well. Add hot cream mix to the bowl and whisk. Add liquid back to the pot and stir over a low heat to thicken. When the custard coats the back of your spoon, it's cooked. Churn in an ice cream machine and store in freezer until ready to serve.

To plate Place a circle cutter in the centre of the plate. Place the trout into the cutter, and using a spoon lightly press down evenly. Add the cucumber on top of the tartar, overlapping the whole way around to complete a circle. Rocher the wasabi ice cream with a tea spoon in the centre. Grate the egg yolk on top of the filling (only inside the cutter) wipe the excess off the plate. Add the dill oil to the outside of the cutter. Then carefully lift the cutter up and off the plate. Serve.

< Sea trout tartar, cucumber, apple, dill and wasabi ice cream

Page 136 Butter poached brill, tartare sauce, pomme anna

Mullygarry Farm lamb-cannon, shank and shoulder, salt baked beetroot, sweet potato purée, braising sauce

Ingredients

Cannon

Cannon of lamb - 500g

Garlic - 1 clove

Rosemary - 10g

Thyme - 10g

Shoulder and shank

Lamb shoulder - 700g

Lamb hind shank - 1

Red wine - 1l

Carrot - 1

Leek - 1

Celery - 2 sticks

Onion - 1

Bay leaf - 2

Balsamic vinegar - 100ml

Salt - 20g

Port - 200mls

Garlic - 4 cloves

Rosemary - 2 stalks

Chicken stock - 2l

Beetroot

Beetroots - 2

Rock salt - 200g

Sweet potato purée

Sweet potatoes - 2 large

Chicken stock - 500ml

Double cream - 50ml

Rock salt

Potatoes

Jersey Royal potatoes - 4

Lamb fat - 1l

Lamb sauce

Madira - 50ml

Redcurrent jelly

Method

Serves 4

Cannon Marinade in finely chopped garlic, rosemary and thyme for 1 hr. Season with rock salt. Roast in a pan with foaming butter until golden brown. Put into the oven at 180°C for 4 mins or until the cannon is 45°C in the centre. Rest for 10 mins. Reheat for 1 min and carve.

Shank and shoulder Cut shoulder in chunks and roast in a pan. Roast off the shank in the same pan until brown. Add both into a metal container suitable for an oven. Using the same pan add the chopped veg and herbs and roast off. Add wine and burn off the alcohol. Add the stock and remaining ingredients to the container. Cover in tin foil and place in an oven at 140°C for 4 hours until soft and tender.

When cool place shoulder in a vac pack bag all together, and vac down tight. Roll with a rolling pin until flat and rest in fridge. When cold and set cut into fingers and sear on each side in a pan and add some of the braising stock to glaze. Finish with a metal skewer and grated almond.

Pick down the shank removing bones and cartilage. Add a little braising stock and slowly cook in a pan until sticky and soft. Season to taste ready to top the confit potatoes.

Salt baked beetroot On a tray place 2 tbsp full of rock salt and place the beetroots on top. Place into an oven at 180°C for 45 mins until soft. Peel and cut into wedges. Warm up in a pan with butter.

Sweet potato purée In a pan roast off peeled and diced sweet potato and salt. Add stock and cook until soft. Add cream and reduce. Blend until smooth (add cold butter if needed). Season to taste.

Lamb fat potato Top and tail jersey royals leaving a thick centre wedge. Roast each side in a pan with some lamb fat, salt and some butter. Cover in lamb fat and place in an oven at 150°C for 30 mins or until tender. Take out and place some shank on top with a little micro leaf for presentation.

To plate Serve both potato and pressed shoulder on side plates or on a nice little box filled with pebbles. Spoon sweet potato purée onto a plate just off-centre. Place lamb loin in the centre, beside the purée. Add two chunks of beetroot either side of lamb. Pour jus to the side of the lamb.

< Mullygarry Farm lamb-cannon, shank and shoulder, salt baked beetroot, sweet potato purée

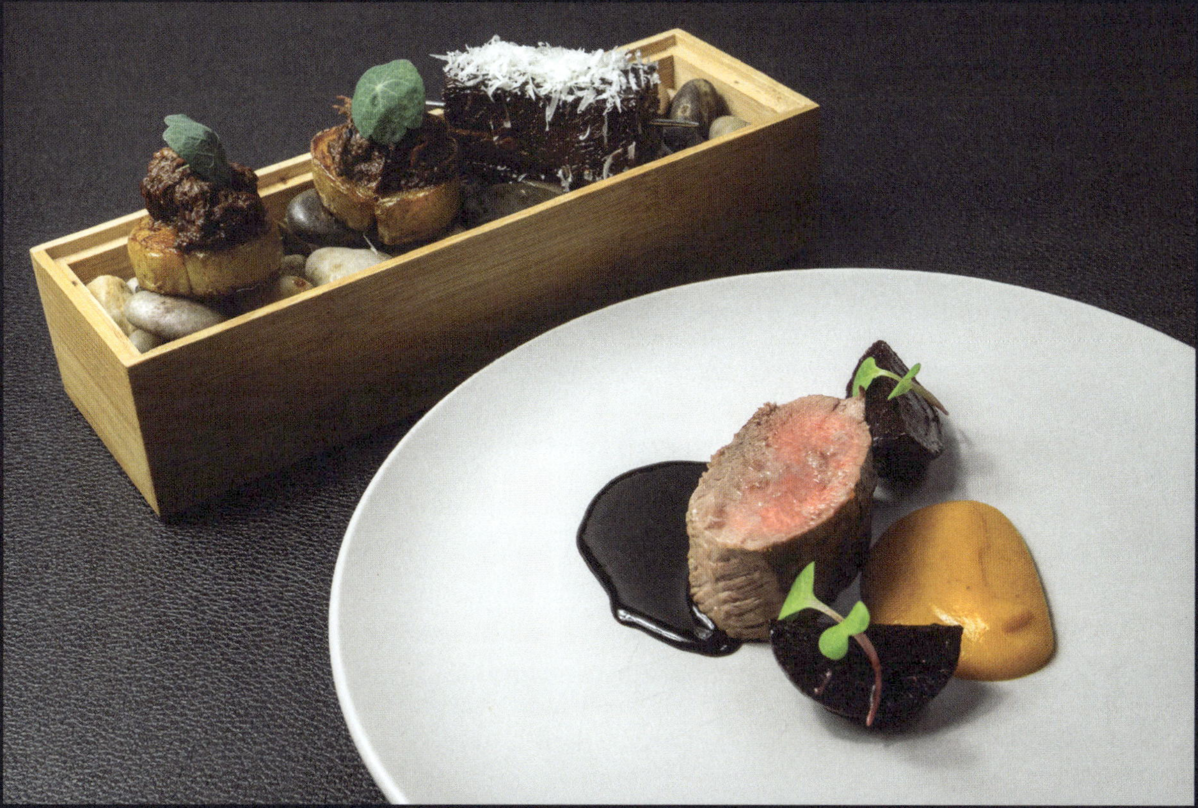

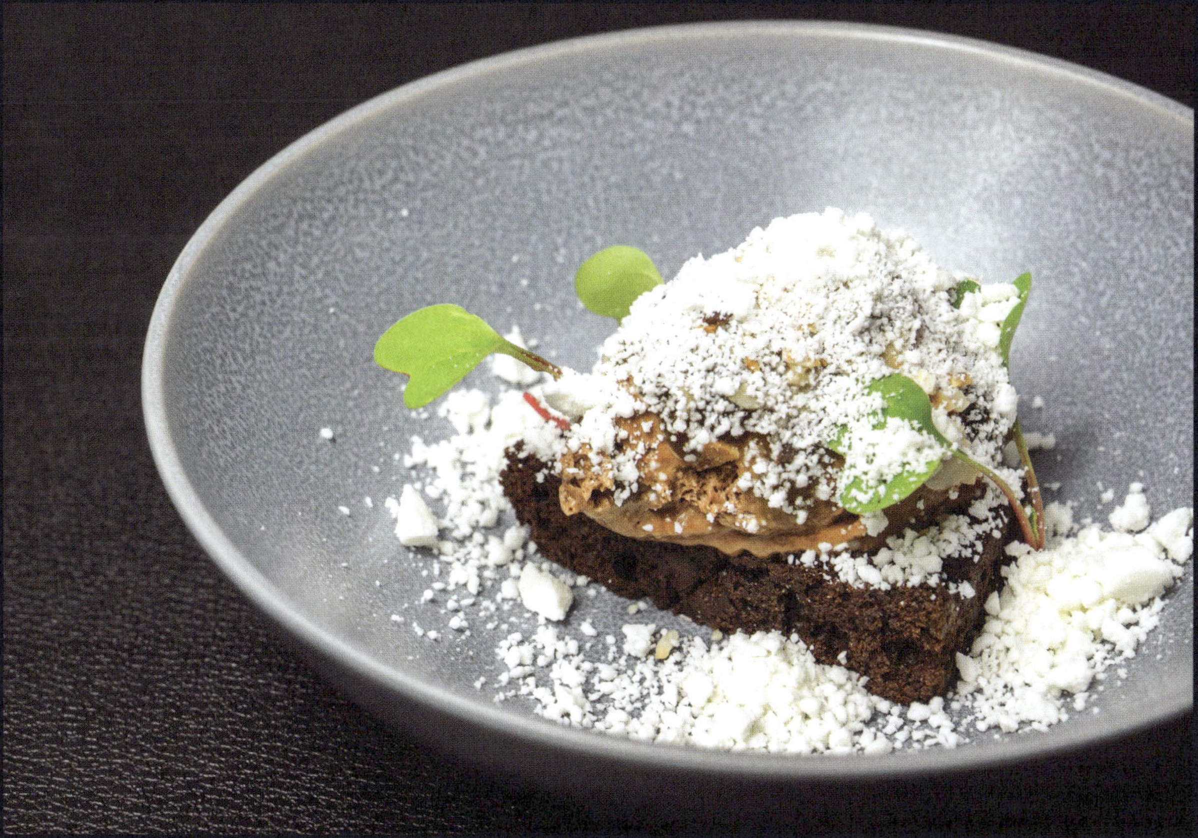

Page 137 Milk chocolate mousse, dark chocolate brownie, roasted pistachios,

Butter poached brill, tartare sauce, pomme anna

Ingredients

Brill

Brill - 4 x 100g portions
Butter - 400g
Dulse - 40g
Chicken stock - 200ml

Tartare sauce

Shallots - 2
Garlic - 1 clove
Sauvignon blanc - 250ml
Chicken stock - 300ml
Double cream - 100ml
Dill - 10g
Capers - 20
Gerkin - 1 medium

Pomme anna

Potatoes - 5 large roosters
Clarified butter - 1l
Sea salt - 20g

Method

Serves 4

Brill Fillet whole brill, take off skin and portion into 100g portions. In a metal container or water bath place butter, stock and dulse together and heat to 80°C. Poach brill for 12 mins. Take out and rest before serving on a dry cloth to clear off excess butter.

Sauce In a pan add oil, sliced shallots and sliced garlic. Cook until soft without colour. Add white wine and reduce by 2/3. Add chicken stock and reduce by half. Add cream and reduce again until sauce is at the correct consistency. Finish with chopped dill, finely diced gerkin and capers. Adjust salt if required.

Pomme anna Preheat oven to 180°C. Peel the potatoes and slice them very thinly (about 1.5mm thick) using a mandoline or sharp knife. Butter the pan. Brush the bottom and sides of the skillet with some of the melted butter. Layer the potatoes. Arrange one layer of overlapping potato slices in a circular pattern at the bottom of the skillet (this will be the top when flipped). Brush with butter, season lightly with salt and pepper. Repeat with the remaining potatoes, butter, salt, and pepper until all are used. Bake in the oven for 45 mins. Remove from oven. You want a tight, compact cake. Place a plate or pan on top with some weight and let it sit for 1 hr. Then place in fridge until cold and set. Cut into fingers and fry until golden on both sides.

To plate Place the pomme anna in middle of the plate, and spoon the sauce around it. Place fish on top of potato. Garnish the top of sauce with some micro herbs like red vain sorrel or chervil.

Milk chocolate mousse, dark chocolate brownie, roasted pistachios, tarragon and mint ketchup, frozen goats cheese snow

Ingredients

Chocolate cake

All-purpose flour - 60g

Unsweetened cocoa powder - 25g

Baking powder - 1/2 tsp

Salt - 1/4 tsp

Unsalted butter - 60g. Softened

Caster sugar - 100g

Egg - 1 large

Vanilla extract- 1/2 tsp

Milk - 60ml

Roasted pistachio

Pistachio - 50g

Icing sugar - 20g

Chocolate mousse

Dark chocolate (around 60 – 70% cocoa) - 100g

Milk - 2 tbsp

Sugar - 2 tbsp. Or to taste

Egg whites - 3 large. At room temperature

Whipping cream - 120ml

Salt - A pinch

Goats cheese snow

Fivemile town goats cheese - 500g

Tarragon and mint ketchup

Tarragon - 100g

Mint - 100g

Water - 100ml

Caster sugar - 50g

White wine vinegar - 10ml

Ultratex - 10g

Method

Serves 4

Chocolate cake Preheat oven to 175°C. Grease and flour a 15cm round cake pan or line it with parchment paper. In a bowl, sift together the flour, cocoa powder, baking powder and salt. In another bowl, beat the butter and sugar until light and fluffy (about 2 – 3 mins).

Add egg and vanilla. Mix in the egg and vanilla extract until combined. Combine wet and dry. Add the dry ingredients to the wet mixture in two batches, alternating with the milk. Mix until just combined. Pour the batter into the prepared pan. Bake for 20 – 25 mins, or until a toothpick inserted in the center comes out clean. Let the cake cool in the pan for 10 mins, then transfer to a wire rack to cool completely.

Roasted pistachio Pre heat oven at 180°C. Sieve icing sugar on top and roll. Roast in oven for a few mins until golden shaking every 2 mins to completely carmelise all over. Take out and let cool.

Goats cheese snow Cut goats cheese into small dice and lay flat on a tray lined with parchment paper so the cheese doesn't stick. Freeze over night. Blend in a high powered blender like a Thermomix in small amounts. Store in an air tight container in the freezer until ready to serve.

Tarragon and mint ketchup Pick all the leaves of mint and tarragon. Add water, sugar, vinegar to a pan and heat to 85°C. Add herbs and cook for 20 secs. Blend until smooth. Pass through a sieve and muslin cloth (let the liquid pass slowly – don't force it). In a bowl add the green liquid and ultratex together and whisk until gel consistency. Add a pinch of salt to season.

Chocolate mousse Break chocolate into small pieces and melt gently with milk in a heatproof bowl over a pot of simmering water (double boiler). Stir until smooth. Let it cool slightly, then stir in vanilla extract if using. In a clean bowl, beat egg whites with a pinch of salt until soft peaks form.

Gradually add sugar and continue beating until stiff peaks form. In another bowl, whip the cream until soft peaks form. Don't over-whip. First, mix a spoonful of the whipped egg whites into the chocolate to lighten it. Then gently fold in the rest of the egg whites. Finally, fold in the whipped cream. Chill for at least 2 hrs before serving in a container ready to quenelle.

To serve Place cake in centre of a bowl. Rocher the mousse on top. Pipe ketchup over the mousse. Add some sorrel. Spoon over frozen goats cheese snow on top and around the sides.

16

Artis
Phelim O'Hagan
Head chef owner

Artis is a high-end dining restaurant in the heart of Derry City - serving modern Irish Cuisine using the best quality Irish ingredients, all sourced from local suppliers, fisheries, farms or foraged from the surrounding area.

My love for hospitality began when I was 14; still at school I took up a part time job as a kitchen porter, at Harry's Bar & Restaurant just on the border of Derry and Donegal. It was one of the few restaurants in the area in those days that used fresh Irish ingredients and cooked everything from scratch. It was a great foundation for me, and I stayed there for five years during which time I also attended Catering College in Killybegs.

I moved to Ardmore, Waterford to work in the One Star Michelin Cliff Restaurant in the Cliff House Hotel. I worked there for two years with some fantastic chefs and gained a wealth of knowledge and skill which allowed me to make the move to Scotland to work under Andrew Fairlie at Gleneagles.

I spent a year there and in April 2014 I came home to settle down and took up the position of Head Chef at Browns Bonds Hill, which was the only fine dining restaurant in town then. During that time, I took part in Great British Menu 2021 and was the Northern Ireland Finalist.

After ten years at Browns, I thought the time was right to move on and opened Artis in November 2021.

Artis is Latin for "craft" and is in Derry's "craft village" of restored 18th-to-19th century thatched houses and cobbled streets containing many craft shops that attract tourists and local people. The restaurant is relaxed and unassuming with soft furnishings, calm lighting and walls covered in artwork of nearby beaches, the surrounding area and caricatures of famous County Derry people.

We serve people food they recognise but by using both traditional and modern techniques, we find creative ways to maximise the full potential of each ingredient to make it taste better and definitely not what they expect.

One of our most popular dishes is a Derry salad which is a take on a nostalgic classic of most Irish households – ours comes with an Irish Ham & Smoked Cheese Croquette, accompanied by organic beetroot, pickled onion, salad cream and local grown salad leaves. A simple dish but infinitely enhanced.

Opening Artis was a huge challenge, but I was greatly helped by my first head chef at Harry's, Ray Moran, who was my initial business partner. Now I run the restaurant with my partner and restaurant manager Serina and fellow chef Kevin. I've got a great team around me; we are passionate in what we do – our love for championing Irish ingredients and exceptional hospitality.

The whole dining scene in Northern Ireland and Derry has dramatically changed and flourished in the last ten years and it's great to see Artis play a part in that.

"We find creative ways to maximise the full potential of each ingredient to make it taste better."

Phelim's Derry salad

Ingredients

Smoked cheddar and ham croquette

Smoked Applewood cheese - 500g. Grated

Cooked Irish ham - 500g. Chopped

Parmesan - 100g. Grated

Plain flour - 100g

Unsalted butter - 100g

Milk - 1l. Warmed

Dijon mustard - 1 tbsp

Worcestershire sauce - 1 tbsp

Salt and pepper

Salad cream

Egg yolks - 4. Hard boiled

English mustard - 4 tbsp

White wine vinegar - 6 tbsp

Sugar - 50g

Rapeseed Oil - 300ml

Double cream - 300ml

Lemon - 1/2. Juice

Salt and pepper

Pickled red onion

Red onion - 1

Red wine vinegar - 200g

Sugar - 200g

Water - 100g

Star anise - 2

Bay leaf - 1

Peppercorns - 4

Thyme - 1 sprig

Garlic - 1 clove. Halved

Salad garnish

Baby gem lettuce - 1

Lolla rossa or other salad leaves

Fresh Herbs of choice

Beetroot - 1. Thinly sliced

Hard boiled eggs - 6

Method

Serves 4

This is our twist on the very nostalgic Irish summertime salad of our childhood. All the ingredients are what remind me of the version we make in Derry.

Smoked cheddar and ham croquette Start by making a Roux. Melt the butter in a large pot and then add in the flour and cook on a low heat for 3 – 4 mins, stirring constantly. Add the lightly warmed milk bit by bit, stirring it into the roux – it should be smooth and glossy. Remove from the heat and stir in the Applewood, parmesan, Irish ham, mustard, Worcestershire sauce and salt and pepper.

Set in a tray at least 2.5cm deep, lined with cling film or greaseproof paper. Transfer mix to freezer until its partially frozen, i.e. firm enough to cut to desired shape (use cookie cutters or simply cut into rectangles). Refreeze until solid.

Now bread the croquette by rolling lightly in flour, then in the egg wash, then breadcrumbs. Repeat this process 3 times. Set aside for frying (can be stored in freezer for up to 1 month).

Fry croquette in deep fat fryer at 180°C until golden brown. Turn down to 160°C for 8 mins. Once heated this can be pierced with a food probe (through the top so it doesn't leak). It should be 70°C.

Salad cream Put hard boiled yolks, mustard, vinegar and sugar in a blender. Blend and slowly pour in the oil until combined and smooth. Add cream while blending and blend for a further 5 – 10 secs. Season with lemon juice and salt and pepper. Then transfer to a piping bag.

Pickled red onions Prepare this 24 hrs in advance. Mix all ingredients except the onion in a pot and bring to the boil. Remove from the heat. Half and peel the red onion, cut each half into segments through the core and add to the warm pickle. Set aside and allow to cool before serving.

Salad garnish Wash and dry all leaves and herbs that you have decided to use (we use baby gem, lolla rossa and foraged herbs and flowers available to us daily). Cut or pick these into desired size (remove stems etc), and dress with rapeseed oil. Thinly slice Beetroot and store in ice water. Boil eggs in boiling water for 10 mins, put in ice water to cool and set aside to be shelled before serving.

To serve

In the centre of the plate add a dollop of the salad cream and add the croquette on top. Assemble the salad leaves and herbs, beetroot discs and hard boiled eggs as desired around the croquette and finish with more salad cream if desired.

< Phelim's Derry salad

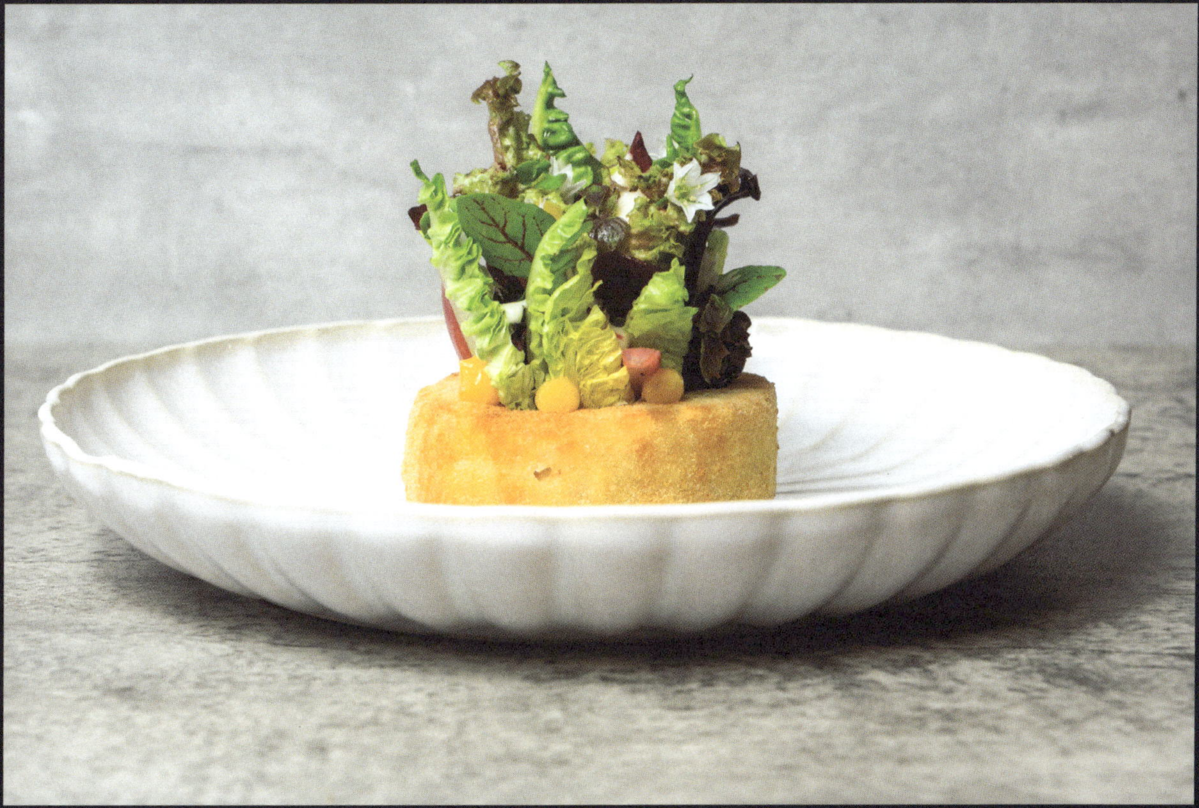

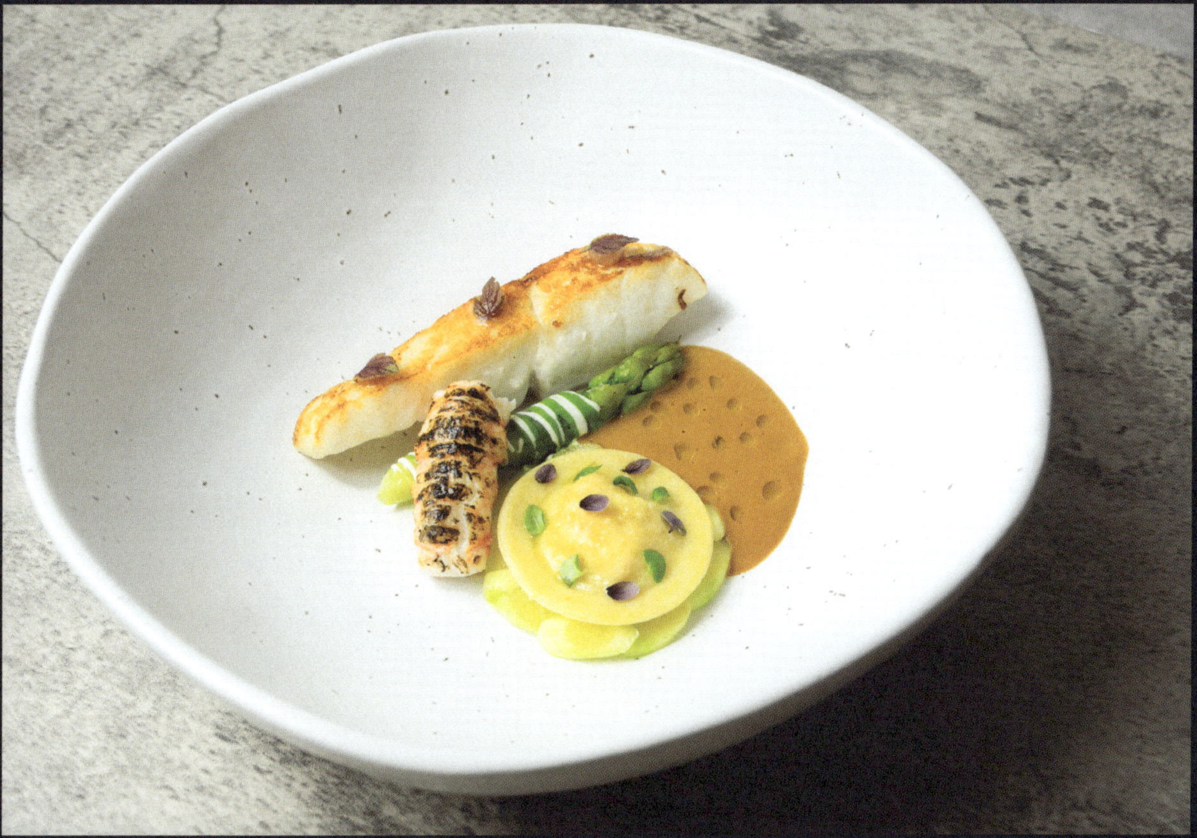

Page 144 Wild turbot, asparagus, langoustine bisque

Pine nut baked scallops with white asparagus, morel mushrooms and Pedro Ximénez

Ingredients

Scallops

Scallops - 8 large. Cleaned – your fish monger can do this

Pine nut butter

Pine nuts - 200g. Roughly chopped

Shallot - 1. Diced

Lemon zest - 1/2 tsp

Coriander seeds - 1/2 tsp

Fennel seeds - 1/2 tsp

Butter - 250g. Salted

Breadcrumbs - 25g

Salt and pepper

Pedro Ximénez gel

Pedro Ximénez sherry - 250ml

Agar agar - 3g. Natural thickening agent

Agrodolce (sweet and sour)

Pine nuts - 300g

Shallots - 300g. Sliced

Sugar - 80g

Balsamic vinegar - 250g

Seasoned white asparagus

White asparagus - 4 spears

Water - 500ml

Unsalted butter - 100g

Bay leaves - 2

Thyme - 1 sprig

Salt and white peppercorns - 1 tsp

White asparagus Espuma

Reserved liquid from braised asparagus

Whipping cream - 100ml

Lemon - Zest of 1

Morel mushrooms

Fresh or dried morels - 12

Shallot - 1

Garlic - 1 clove

Butter - 20g

Method

This dish is a symphony of seasonal delicacies, beautifully paired with local scallops – rich, sweet, salty, sour and earthy. A flavour packed combination.

Pine nut butter Beat all ingredients until combined. Roll into a cylinder using parchment paper. Chill until firm. Then cut into thin discs. Place one disc on each seasoned scallop. Set aside until ready to cook.

Pedro Ximénez gel Whisk the agar agar into Pedro Ximénez and bring to a boil. Chill completely. Blend until smooth. Pass through a sieve and transfer to a piping bag.

Agrodolce Combine all ingredients in a saucepan. Simmer gently until thick and sticky.

Seasoned white asparagus Peel asparagus from just below the tip to the base; reserve peelings. Cut off bases and reserve trimmings. Add all ingredients to a pot. Submerge the asparagus. Cover with parchment and peelings. Simmer for 10 – 15 mins until tender. Remove asparagus. Reserve liquid, peelings, and trimmings.

White asparagus Espuma Add cream and lemon zest to reserved liquid and boil for 2 mins. Blend until smooth. Pass through a sieve, and season. Transfer to an Espuma gun and charge with 2 charges, then set aside for later (if you don't have an Espuma gun skip this step and use as a sauce)

Morel mushrooms Clean and dry the mushrooms. If using dried mushrooms, rehydrate in boiling water, drain and pat dry. Melt butter in a pan over medium heat. Add the chopped shallots and garlic. Sauté for 2 – 3 mins. Season and keep warm.

To serve Bake Scallops with pine nut butter for 5 mins at 175°C. Pipe Pedro Ximénez gel onto plates. Lay one Asparagus spear in the center. Divide the scallops and morels around the plate. Add a quenelle of agrodolce on the side. Add Espuma (or sauce) to finish. Finish with fresh herbs to garnish (I personally prefer Wild Garlic).

< Pine nut baked scallops with white asparagus, morel mushrooms and Pedro Ximénez

Wild turbot, asparagus, langoustine bisque

Ingredients

Fish and shellfish

Wild turbot - 4 fillets

Whole langoustines - 4. Shells and heads reserved

Fish brine

Water - 1l

Sea salt - 100g

Lemon - 1/2. Sliced

Cloves - 2

Star anise - 2

Langoustine bisque

White wine - 400ml

Fish stock - 800ml

Shallots - 2. Chopped

Garlic - 1 clove. Chopped

Carrot - 1. Chopped

Celery - 1 stick. Chopped

Fennel - 1/2 bulb. Chopped

Butter - 80g

Bay Leaf - 1

Thyme - 1 sprig

Tomato purée - 1 tbsp

Brandy - 100ml

Cream - 300ml

Lemon - 1. Juice

Star anise - 4

Pasta for ravioli

'00' Flour - 250g

Egg yolks - 6

Whole egg - 1

Rapeseed oil - 30ml

To garnish

XL asparagus spears - 4. Or 8 regular spears

Crème fraîche - 100g

Method

Serves 4

At Artis, we pride ourselves on using only the finest wild fish. Turbot and langoustine are real delicacies – simple to prepare, yet luxurious in flavour. It pairs beautifully with the rich bisque and fresh asparagus.

Turbot Prepare the brine by combining all ingredients in a saucepan. Bring to a boil, then cool completely. Submerge Turbot fillets in the cooled brine for 15 mins. Remove, pat dry, and refrigerate uncovered until ready to cook.

Langoustines Remove the heads from the tails by gently pulling apart. Peel the tails and set aside. Reserve the shells, heads, and claws. Crack the claws with a knife and remove the meat (if your Langoustines are big enough). Keep all meat chilled and reserve the shells and heads for the bisque.

Langoustine bisque In a large pan, melt the butter and sweat shallots, garlic, carrot, celery and fennel until soft. Add the langoustine shells and heads. Cook for 5 mins until slightly browned. Stir in tomato purée and cook for 2 mins. Deglaze with brandy, then add white wine, fish stock, herbs, spices, and lemon juice. Simmer for 30 – 40 mins.
Strain into a clean pan, discard solids, add cream, and reduce to desired consistency. Season to taste.

Langoustine ravioli Make the pasta by placing flour in a food processor. Add egg yolks and whole eggs. Blend slowly while drizzling in rapeseed oil until the dough comes together. Remove from the processor. Knead for 3 – 4 mins. Then wrap in cling film and rest for 30 mins.

For the filling Finely chop the claw meat and mix in a bowl with a little crème fraîche, zest from 1/2 lemon, salt and pepper.
Roll the pasta using a pasta machine. Cut 8 discs approximately 5cm in diameter. Place 1 tbsp of filling on 4 discs. Lightly wet the edges with water. Top with remaining discs, and press gently to seal tight, removing any air. Set Ravioli aside in the fridge until ready to cook.

To assemble the dish Place a pot of salted water on to boil for asparagus and ravioli. Put a pan with some vegetable oil on medium heat. Once hot, cook turbot for 2 – 3 mins each side or until core temperature reaches 40°C.

Baste with butter and let rest for 1 min. Set aside. Boil ravioli and asparagus for 3 mins. Remove and dress asparagus with rapeseed oil, salt, crème fraîche, and fine herbs.

Garnish ravioli with rapeseed oil, salt, and micro basil. Warm langoustine bisque and plate all ingredients. Finish the langoustine tail by blow-torching and top the dish.

Tirami-soufflé™

Ingredients

Soufflé mix
Brewed coffee - 180ml
Tia Maria - 45ml
Marsala wine/port - 10ml
Cornflour - 15g

Meringue
Egg whites - 2
Sugar - 75g

Ramekins prep
Butter - 50g
Sugar - 50g
Cocoa powder - 50g

Coffee custard
Milk - 300ml
Cream - 300ml
Egg yolks - 140g
Sugar - 70g
Vanilla pod - 1. Seeds
Tia Maria - To taste
Marsala wine - To taste

Mascarpone ice cream
Milk - 250g
Mascarpone cheese - 350g
Egg yolks - 200g
Sugar - 150g

Chocolate tuille
Melted butter - 50g
Egg whites - 50g
Ground almonds - 50g
Plain flour - 50g
Cocoa powder - 10g

Method

Serves 4

In the restaurant, I love to experiment – especially with desserts. This creation brings together two beloved classics, the soufflé and tiramisu, in a playful and unexpected way.

Soufflé mix Boil coffee, Tia Maria, Marsala wine and cornflour together while stirring. When thickened and boiled, transfer to a bowl to cool. Meanwhile, make the meringue. Whip egg whites in electric mixer until doubled in volume. Gradually add sugar and continue whipping until thick and glossy. Once the soufflé base has cooled, whisk together with the meringue in thirds, folding gently. Transfer to a piping bag.

Coffee custard Whisk egg yolks and sugar together. Bring milk, cream, and vanilla seeds to a simmer. Then pour over egg mixture. Transfer everything back to the pan and cook over medium heat until thickened. Pass through a sieve and stir in Tia Maria and Marsala wine to taste. Cool before serving.

Mascarpone ice cream (prepare 24 Hours in advance) Whisk egg yolks and sugar together. Bring milk to a simmer, then pour over egg mixture. Transfer everything back to the pan and cook over medium heat until thickened. Take it off the heat and whisk in Mascarpone. Transfer to ice cream machine and churn until ready.

Chocolate tuille Melt butter and combine with all other ingredients until a paste forms. Spread onto a baking mat using a template or stencil. Bake at 180°C until crisp.

Ramekin prep Butter the ramekins evenly in upward strokes. Coat first with sugar, emptying excess. Repeat with cocoa powder.

Assembly and baking Pipe Soufflé mixture into prepared ramekins, tapping gently to remove air bubbles. Level the tops with an offset spatula and clean rims with a damp cloth. Bake soufflés at 180°C until risen. Once baked, remove and place ramekins on serving plates. Place Tuille on top, scoop ice cream on gently, and serve with coffee custard on the side.

17

Cyprus Avenue
Richard McCracken
Owner

"Cyprus Avenue is a local brasserie you would love to have at the end of your street."

Cyprus Avenue is a modern family run European brasserie restaurant embedded in the local community we serve in East Belfast. We have been lucky enough to be included in the Michelin Guide since our inception in 2016.

I began scrubbing pots in my local pub when I was at school and quickly enjoyed the buzz of a busy kitchen. After university in Glasgow, I went to work for Tom Kitchin at his eponymous Edinburgh restaurant. From there I went to work for Helene Darroze on the Rue d'assas in Paris and finally the late Andrew Fairlie at Gleneagles. Living and breathing all things hospitality during this time gave me a fantastic grounding in the graft, sacrifice and discipline required to succeed in the industry. By the time I opened Cyprus Avenue in 2016 I just hoped I had gained enough experience to open my own restaurant.

Cyprus Avenue is family oriented. We think of it as a local brasserie you would love to have at the end of your street. The restaurant is open throughout the day, seven days a week for breakfast, lunch and dinner. It is important that it's accessible to everybody for a variety of occasions: a coffee, business meeting or a family in for Sunday lunch.

We doubled the size of the restaurant at the end of 2018 and just as we were finding our feet with the expansion- covid struck. Like every other restaurant this came as an absolute shock to the system, but we were determined to stay in business. We opened a corner shop in the restaurant selling local produce and converted a three-wheeler van into a takeaway pizza truck. Basically, we would have cut your hedge to keep ourselves busy!

There were many benefits to our covid endeavours; it gave our suppliers an outlet for their produce, and I think the local community enjoyed a browse. A lot of the guests who used us over covid are now part of the loyal customer base that we are blessed with at Cyprus Avenue. It also gave us a clear direction during that period which I feel was important.

Our team at Cyprus Avenue hails from around the globe and it is very much more than the sum of its parts. We draw inspiration from each other's varied experiences and inherited gastronomy to ensure the menu is constantly evolving. Our menu is dictated by the seasons and rooted in the use of produce from local suppliers renowned for the freshness and quality of their products which we are so fortunate to have in Northern Ireland.

There is an innate warmth and genuine hospitality in the people of Northern Ireland and in particular historically industrial working-class East Belfast. This is personified by our staff at Cyprus Avenue who bust a gut to spoil guests and love sharing their special occasions.

I'm very pleased that Cyprus Avenue has become an important part of the community.

Scallops, chicory croissant, poached egg and black pudding

Ingredients

Ready to roll croissant dough - 1 pack

Black pudding - 1 log. From your local butcher

Free range eggs - 5 large. 1 egg is for egg wash

Red chicory - 1 pack

Baby gem - 1 head

Caster sugar

Apple - 1. For garnish

Scallops - 6 large. From local fish supplier

Blue poppy seeds

Pumpkin seeds

Sesame seeds

Butter - 1 knob. For cooking scallops

Oil

Salad dressing

Dijon mustard - 1 tsp

Sherry vinegar - 1 tbsp

Egg yolk - 1

Olive oil - 6 tbsp. Use good quality

Salt and pepper

Method

Salad dressing To make your salad dressing start by separating the egg white from the yolk. In a large bowl place the mustard and egg yolk and whisk vigorously. While whisking, add 1 tbsp of olive oil at a time. Take care to make sure all the oil is emulsified before adding the next spoonful. Add in the sherry vinegar and season with salt and pepper.

Croissant building To make the croissant filling firstly take your chicory and remove the outer leaves and split down the middle and remove the centre core. Rinse under water. Take the outer leaves and core and chop into small pieces and place into a pan with 2 tbsp of sugar, 2 tbsp of water and 1 tsp of coffee granules. Place the pan onto a medium heat and cook until the sugar becomes a caramel and the chicory trim has broken down. This should take around 10 mins. Set this aside it will be your filling for the croissant. To build the croissant, cut the pastry into 4 large triangles – around 7cm at the base and 15cm long. Place a spoonful of jam at the bottom and roll into a nice croissant shape. Don't worry about the jam spilling out slightly. Place the croissants onto a greased baking tray and brush with beaten egg and sprinkle with blue poppy seeds, sesame seeds and pumpkin seeds. Bake in a preheated oven at 180°C for 14 mins.

Poached egg method To poach your eggs, place a medium sized saucepan half filled with water and a good splash of vinegar onto a high heat and bring to the boil. Once boiled, turn the heat down slightly and use a whisk in a circular motion to create a whirlpool. Carefully crack your eggs into the water and cook for 3 – 4 mins until the white is firm. Carefully remove the eggs from the water with a slotted spoon. Trim eggs with scissors before serving.

For the scallops Carefully take your scallops and cut down the middle lengthwise. We cut the scallops like this so it has a nice flat surface area to get a lovely even roast. To cook place a large non stick frying pan on high heat. Take your scallops and on the flat side season well with salt and pepper and dress with oil. When your pan is up to temperature carefully place them into the pan flat side down in a clockwise motion and roast for 1 min. Then add your butter and let the scallops roast for 30 secs. Remove the pan from the heat and very carefully flip your scallops and leave them in the pan for a further 30 secs to cook the other side. Remove from the pan and serve immediately.

To garnish Take 1 head of baby gem and cut into long strips and rinse under water, in a bowl place your baby gem and chicory leaves and dress with salad dressing. Place the scallops on top. Finish the dish with freshly cut apple sticks.

< Scallops, chicory croissant, poached egg and black pudding

Page 150 Venison loin, blueberry, braised red cabbage, sticky faggot and ricotta dumplings

Venison loin, blueberry, braised red cabbage, sticky faggot and ricotta dumplings

Ingredients

For the venison loin

Venison loin - 1kg. Please speak to your local butcher ask for bones if possible to make stock and jus

Venison stock bones - 2kg

Onions - 3. Unpeeled and halved

Garlic - 1 head. Unpeeled and halved

Bouquet garni - Large. Made with fresh rosemary, fresh thyme, fresh parsley and bay

Leeks - 2. Halved

Carrots - 2. Halved

Celery - 1 stalk. Roughly chopped

Sea salt - 1 tsp

Whole peppercorns - 1 tbsp

Blueberry powder

Fresh blueberries - 125g

Juniper berries - 2

Icing sugar - 200g

For braised red cabbage

Red cabbage - 1 head

Red wine - 200ml

Red wine vinegar - 100ml

Brown sugar - 4 tbsp

Star anise - 1

Juniper berries - 2

Cinnamon stick - 1

Oil for roasting

Salt and pepper

Method

For the venison loin Preheat the oven to 200°C. Place the bones in a roasting tray with the onions and garlic roast for around 45 mins until brown.

Transfer the roasted bones, onions and garlic to a large stockpot and fill with 4l of cold water. Cover and bring to a simmer. Add the bouquet garni, leeks, carrots, celery, salt and peppercorns. Gently simmer for 6 hrs, skimming off the froth that forms and topping up the water as required. Strain the stock through a fine-mesh sieve, discarding the ingredients.

To then make the jus place the stock into a large pot and cook on a high heat until its reduced down to a thick glossy consistency. Set this aside to glaze up the faggots later on.

For the blueberry powder Start by mixing your blueberries, icing sugar and juniper together in a bowl then place onto an oven tray which is lined with a silicon mat. Bake in a preheated oven at 140°C for 30 mins or until all the berries are broken down. Remove from the oven and mix well with a spatula making sure to scrape all the goodness off the mat. Return to the oven at 60°C for a further 8 hrs. Turn off the oven and leave it overnight to dry out. The next day place your blueberries into a food processor and blend into a powder. Store in an airtight container.

For the venison loin Take venison loin and dress with a tbsp of vegetable oil, then season with salt and black pepper. Heat a large heavy-based frying pan until very hot. Sear the fillet on all sides until dark golden-brown on the outside (this will take about 3 mins). Then reduce the heat to low and gently fry adding a knob of butter and turning regularly, for 6 – 8 mins for medium rare. Set the loin aside for 10 mins to rest before carving. Place your venison loin into blueberry powder and roll until fully coated. Then carve.

For the red cabbage Quarter the red cabbage and remove the core, and shred into fine strips. Into a large pan place a good amount of oil and place on a medium – high heat. Place your cabbage into the pan and begin to roast continually, stirring with a wooden spoon. The cabbage should take around 10 mins to roast and start to soften. Once the cabbage has cooked down then add the red wine, red wine vinegar, sugar, star anise, juniper and cinnamon. Give this all a good mix and bring to a simmer. Lower the heat and place a lid on top and cook for around 2 hrs stirring occasionally.

For the sage and ricotta dumplings Start by bringing a large sauce pan of water to the boil and have a bowl with some cold water and ice to refresh your spinach. When the water comes to a boil, season with salt. Carefully place all the spinach into the pot for 30 secs. Remove the spinach using a slotted spoon into the iced water. Drain the spinach in a sieve and then ring out with a tea towel to remove any excess water. Then chop. Keep the pot of water for later.

Sage and riccota dumplings

Olive oil - 1 tbsp. Good quality

Sage leaves - 6 large.Chopped

Ricotta cheese - 325g

Parmesan cheese - 75g

Bread crumbs - 50g

Eggs - 2 large

Polenta - 2 tbsp. Keep aside 1 tbsp for dusting

Spinach - 500g

Salt and pepper

Sticky faggot

Venison mince - 100g

Pork mince - 80g

Chicken livers - 50g. Chopped finely

Prunes - 30g. Chopped finely

Red onion - 1. Finely diced

Garlic - 1 clove. Grated

Barley - 50g

Rosemary - 1 sprig. Chopped

Savoy cabbage leaves - 3 large

Crepenette - Ask your local butcher for a small amount around 100g

Salt and pepper

Veg oil for cooking

Diced veg mix

Celery sticks - 4. Diced

Celeriac - 1 small head. Diced

Large carrots - 2. Diced

To make the dumpling Mix in a large bowl place spinach, oil, both cheeses, chopped sage, breadcrumbs, eggs, 1 tbsp of polenta and season with salt and pepper. By hand mix well until the mix is fully combined then shape into 30g balls and refrigerate for 1 hr until firm. Bring the water back to a boil and prepare to cook. Remove the dumplings from the fridge and place onto a tray and cover with the remaining polenta and roll the balls around to ensure an even coating. To cook carefully drop the balls into the boiling water until they float. This should take around 2 mins to cook. Cook the mix in 2 batches. Once the balls have floated, remove from the heat and allow to cool. To finish off the dumplings, cook in oil at 160°C until golden brown in colour.

Cooking the barley Place the barley into a heavy based sauce pan then place into a preheated oven at 180°C for 30 mins stirring every ten minutes to achieve an even toasting. Once roasted, remove from the oven and place on the stove cover with chicken stock and bring to a medium heat. Cook until tender. This should take around 25 – 30 mins. Season well during cooking with salt and pepper. After the barley is cooked, strain off and discard the liquid.

Place crepenette into a bowl of cold water to rinse off any impurities soaking will make it easy to work with.

For the savoy cabbage Blanch in boiling water, seasoned well with salt for 30 secs, remove the cabbage and refresh in cold water and set aside.

To prepare the faggots Place all of the above ingredients into a bowl and mix until fully combined. Roll your venison mixture into a sausage shape and set aside.

On a chopping board or bench place out the crepenette, apply the blanched savoy cabbage leaves. Place your venison sausage mix in the middle and roll up so it's fully covered. Place your sausage into the reduced stock and cook for 4 mins then rotate in the liquor and cook for a further 4 mins. Remove sausage and with a sharp serrated knife cut into 4 pieces for serving keep the reduced stock for saucing your plate.

To prepare the diced vegetables start by taking your vegetables and give them a good rinse under cold water to remove any dirt. Using a vegetable peeler peel the skin off the celeriac and carrots. With a sharp cook knife cut your vegetables into even strips then dice into small chunks. Mix all your diced vegetables together and place into a sauce pan with oil and bring to a medium heat. Cook for around 8 mins, stirring continually until the vegetables start to soften and season well with salt and pepper.

To assemble place red cabbage on base of plate, place venison on top, add sticky faggot, vegetables and finally sauce.

Braised beef ravioli, McCracken's pale ale broth and Hegarty's cheese custard

Ingredients

To make the pasta

Pasta flour - 500g

Egg yolks - 200g

Egg whites - 100g

White vinegar - 2 tbsp

Oil - 2 tbsp

Salt - 1/2 tsp

Ravioli filling

Beef cheek - 700g

Red wine - 300ml

Beef stock - 300ml. Good quality

Bay leaves - 2

Tomato purée - 1 tbsp

Thyme - 1 sprig

Oil for roasting

McCracken's pale ale broth

McCracken's ale - 300ml

Remaining beef cooking liquor

Onion jam

Butter - 1 knob

Red onions - 2 large. Sliced

Red wine - 200ml

Red wine vinegar - 50 ml

Brown sugar - 100g

Salt and pepper

Hegarty's cheese custard

Mature cheddar cheese (such as Hegarty's) - 250g. Grated

Cream cheese - 100g

Double cream - 175ml

Egg yolks - 3

Worcestershire sauce - 4 tbsp

Dijon mustard - 1 tsp

Corn flour - 2 tbsp

Onion rings - to make the batter

Corn flour - 100g

Self-raising flour - 100g

Egg yolk - 1

Sparkling water - 200ml. Chilled

Method

Serves 4

For the pasta Mix all the ingredients together until you obtain a smooth and consistent dough, then knead for 15 mins. Wrap the dough in cling film and leave to rest in the fridge for at least 2 hrs. To make the ravioli, roll out the pasta dough into thin sheets using a pasta machine and cut discs with an 8cm ring.

For the ravioli filling Take your beef cheek, season well and dress with oil then carefully place into a large pan on full heat taking care to achieve an even dark roast on all sides. Remove your beef from the pan and set aside. Place into the pan red wine, beef stock, tomato purée, bay leaves and thyme and bring to the boil. Place beef back in and cook on a low heat with a lid for 2 hrs. Remove the beef from the liquor and place into a bowl and flake apart gently. Reduce the liquor down until it starts to thicken add half of this back into your flaked cheek and mix then form into crescent shapes, place your beef into the fridge until firm.

For McCracken's pale ale broth Place ale into a sauce pan with the remaining beef stock and reduce until sauce becomes thick and shiny.

For the onion jam Melt a knob of butter in a medium pan and add the onions. Add the sugar and seasoning. Lower the heat and simmer for 20 mins giving an occasional stir. Add the vinegar and the red wine. Cook, uncovered, over a low heat with more stirring as necessary until the sauce thickens and bubbles slowly.

For Heggarty's cheese custard Place sauce pan on a medium heat, add cream, mustard, Worcestershire sauce and cream cheese to the pan and bring to a gentle simmer while whisking. Add cornflour to the cheese mixture and continue to whisk, when the mix thickens remove from the heat and add grated cheddar and egg yolks, continue to whisk until all the cheese is fully melted and the mix is thick and glossy.

For the onion rings Place both flours, egg yolk and sparkling water into a bowl and whisk until smooth season with salt & pepper. Peel 1 large red onion and cut into rings. Separate the rings and coat in all purpose flour. Remove the onions from the flour and place into the batter, rotate until fully coated. Deep fry at 180°C until golden brown. Remove from the oil and set aside.

Building the ravioli Place the filling into the middle of the pasta disc. Using a brush with water brush the base layer of pasta then stretch a sheet of pasta over the top and press down firmly to seal. Cook the ravioli in simmering salted water for 2 – 3 mins. Then drain.

To serve Spoon onion jam in the bottom of your bowl, then place warmed ravioli into the sauce and glaze with a spoon, top with onion rings, spoon on cheese sauce and serve with broth and garnish with chives.

Sticky toffee madelines, toffee sauce and salted caramel ice cream

Ingredients

For the madelines
Caster sugar - 280g

Lemon - 1. Zest

Self-raising flour - 315g

Unsalted butter - 325g

Eggs - 8

For the date jam
Pitted dates - 250g

Water - 200ml

Orange - 1. Juice and zest

Lemon - 1. Juice and zest

Brandy or whiskey - A dash

Vanilla pod - 1. Split and seeds released

To finish
Cinnamon sugar - To dust

Icing sugar - 1 tbsp

Cinnamon powder - 1 tsp

Caramel sauce
Caster sugar - 400g

Unsalted butter - 200g

Double cream - 300ml

Sea salt flakes - 1 tsp

For the ice cream
Caster sugar - 3 tbsp

Egg yolks - 7

Full fat milk - 100ml

Double cream - 300ml

Vanilla pod - 1. Split and seeds released

Method

Start by making your date jam Take your dates, orange zest and juice, lemon zest and juice, brandy or whiskey, whole vanilla pod with seeds place all into a sauce pan with the water. Place the pan onto a medium heat and bring to the boil stirring throughout. Once this has boiled, turn the heat to low and cook for 10 – 15 mins until the dates have broken down and the texture is jam-like. Using a stick blender or food processor, blend the mix until smooth. Set the jam aside for later. Take the pieces of butter and place into a sauce pan. Turn the stove heat to medium this ensures the butter cooks evenly. Begin stirring to move the butter around as it melts. Once melted, the butter will begin to foam around the edges. Keep stirring. In about 6 – 8 mins the butter will turn golden brown. The foam will slightly subside and the milk solids on the bottom of the pan will toast. It will smell intensely buttery, nutty, and rich. Remove this from the heat and set aside and keep in the pan so it remains warm.

To assemble the mix Place your flour, sugar and lemon zest into a large mixing bowl. Bring this together with a whisk, when fully mixed, add in your date jam and warm brown butter and whisk again. Then begin mixing in your eggs. Do this one egg at a time until it is fully incorporated. Your mix will look like a thick brown batter. Place the mix into the fridge and let it chill for at least 2 hrs. For cooking remove your mix from the fridge and spoon into a greased madeline tray using 1 large tbsp per mould. Bake in a preheated oven at 160°C for 13 mins. Remove from the oven and allow to cool slightly before removing from the tray. Before serving, dust your madelines with cinnamon powder and icing sugar.

To make the caramel sauce Place a medium-large sized sauce pan onto a medium heat. Start by heating your sugar and 50g of butter together while using a spatula or wooden spoon to stir. Cook this carefully until it starts to turn light brown in colour and you can smell the sugar turning to a caramel. Once this has happened remove the pan from the heat and very carefully add in the double cream. Return the pan to the heat and bring the mix to the boil. Reduce heat to a simmer for a few mins until the sauce starts to thicken. For the last step remove your pan from the heat and whisk in your remaining butter and sea salt flakes.

For the ice cream Heat the cream, milk and vanilla over a low heat in a medium sized saucepan stirring occasionally until it comes to a gentle simmer. Remove from the heat and set aside to allow the vanilla to infuse. In a large mixing bowl whisk together your egg yolks and sugar until pale and thick. Take 1/3 of your cream mixture and whisk it into the eggs and sugar. Place the saucepan back on the heat and bring to the boil then remove from heat and whisk in the egg mixture. Return the pan to a low heat and cook, stirring constantly with a wooden spoon for around 8 – 10 mins paying close attention that the mix does not boil, cook your mix until it is thick enough to coat the back of your wooden spoon. Remove the mix from the heat and place into a large bowl or container and place in the fridge and leave overnight to churn the following day. The following day place your ice cream mix into your ice cream machine and allow it to churn and freeze. Once this process has finished remove from the machine and fold in some of your salted caramel sauce and freeze until serving.

To serve Place madelines on plate alongside ice cream and sauce.

18

UMI
Sean Lafferty
Head chef owner

UMI is an Asian fusion, sushi driven restaurant serving Japanese, Thai and Korean dishes with local ingredients.

My interest in Asian, and particularly Japanese food began when I was head chef of a Japanese chalet restaurant in the Alps. Before then I'd began as a kitchen porter and learned the essential skills of working in a kitchen. I loved the buzz of a kitchen and wanted to be a chef.

I travelled extensively, spending four summers in Ibiza, three winters in Andorra and two years in Austria working in high-end restaurants. I also spent a year working in New Zealand.

I came back to Derry in 2020 and opened a highly successful takeaway sushi outlet that was very popular during covid. As covid restrictions were lifted and the world opened up again I decided to take the next step and open a restaurant. I decided to call it UMI which is a name that resonates both with Japan and the city of Derry as "UMI" means the ocean in Japanese and Derry sits on the edge of the Atlantic Ocean.

At UMI, which is located on the Strand Road in Derry, we bring together Asian and Irish cuisine. We take local produce and ingredients and infuse them with Asian cooking techniques and flavours. As soon as the food's ready we serve it tapas style, so it flows with the emphasis on sharing good, tasty food. As well as tapas we also serve big plates.

All our suppliers and produce are sourced locally, and we change the menu as and when ingredients become available and that of course can be season dependent. When the opportunity arises, we'll change the menu and create a dish. Our main staples are our skilfully rolled sushi

dishes which include crab, beef tempura and salmon. Small plates range from pork belly to duck leg spring roll, tiger prawns and pork dumplings and other offerings. Among the larger plate dishes on offer are a sharing steak or Thai green curry with Pak Choi. We also have a good selection of vegan dishes always available. The staff and I are passionate about our food, and we strive to reflect that passion in the dishes we serve our guests.

We have a great range of drinks and Asian inspired cocktails from local producers and a large selection of wines. There's a lot of energy at UMI and you can enjoy our delicious food and fantastic wines and cocktails while enjoying some good house music under our big disco ball.

Since opening in 2022, we've been very busy and successful. UMI has been so well received, and it's become one of Derry's most popular restaurants with lots of regular customers. We won Best Casual Dining Award in Food and Wine Magazine 2024, and we've received excellent reviews in local media. I'm delighted that UMI has been such a success in Derry.

"At UMI we bring together Asian and Irish cuisine. We take local produce and ingredients and infuse them with Asian cooking techniques and flavours."

Bluefin tuna sushi - 3 ways, nirgiri, tataki and maki

Ingredients

Bluefin tuna nirigi with yuzu gel

Bluefin tuna - 500g. Sushi grade. We use sustainable balfego bluefin

Yuzu juice - 100ml

Ultratex - 4g

Maki topped with spicy bluefin tuna

Sushi rice - 1kg. Premium grade

Nori dried seaweed - 1 sheet. Japanese grade A

Sriacha sauce - Enough to coat the fish

Cucumber - 1. Finely sliced julienne
.

Tataki with citrus and ponzu

Grapefruit - 1

Clementine - 1

Lime - 1

Kitchen blowtorch

Ponzu

Light soy sauce - 40g

Rice vinegar - 50g

Mirin - 10g

Fresh yuzu juice - 15g

Bonito flakes (katsuobushi) - 3g

Method

Serves 4

Nirgiri Wash the sushi rice in bowl or a pot of running cold water. Give the rice a wash with your hand which will result in leaving the water quite cloudy. With a fine sieve drain the water and repeat this process four times until the water eventually becomes clear, and drain until dry. In the bowl of the rice cooker, combine the sushi rice and the water (weighed). Make sure the rice level is flat inside the rice cooker, cook the sushi rice on low for 20 mins. While cooking prepare the rice seasoning. In a small bowl mix the rice vinegar, sugar, mirin and salt until the sugar is dissolved. Once cooked, transfer the sushi rice into a flat bowl or a wooden hangiri if you have one and dress the rice with the seasoning.

On a chopping board with a very sharp knife, thinly slice the tuna against the fiber (lines), at a 45° angle. They should not be too thick or too thin. The size of the cut should be 1/2" wide and 2" long. Have a bowl of lukewarm water – wet your hands and start shaping the rice balls for nigiri. Each rice ball should not exceed 25g. Place the thinly sliced fish in your hand at the base of your fingers and add a small dab of wasabi to the center of fish. Next, place the rice on top of the fish and press down gently. Flip the piece of sushi over so that the fish-side faces up. Repeat the same steps with the remaining ingredients: shape first and cradle, then rotate and serve. In a bowl add your fresh yuzu juice with a whisk, add in your UltraTex and whisk until it turns to a gel. Transfer into a bottle or piping bag and add your dot and serve.

Maki With the remaining sushi rice that has been already cooked, lay out your sheet of nori on a bamboo rolling mat. Fill the nori with a thin layer of sushi rice evenly spread with no lumps and fill it 3/4 of the way to the top. Add your finely sliced cucumbers one inch from the bottom of the sheet. With your hands and thumbs roll the maki as tight as possible but do not squeeze the roll as you can break the rice. Once rolled cut the maki in half then in half again. Use roughly 100g of bluefin tuna. Dice them into roughly 1 cm in size and mix in a bowl with sriracha sauce. Add on top of your cut maki roll and serve.

Tataki With your remaining bluefin, blowtorch on all sides to get an even outer layer. Slice them the same way as nigiri in the paragraph above. For the ponzu add all ingredients into a bowl mix and soak overnight. The next day pass through a fine sieve. Peel your citrus' with a knife and cut into segments.

To serve Put your Ponzu at the bottom of the bowl/plate. Add your cut tuna on top either layered on top of each other or turned into a rose as we have done above. Add your citrus segments and serve.

< Bluefin tuna sushi - 3 ways, nirgiri, tataki and maki

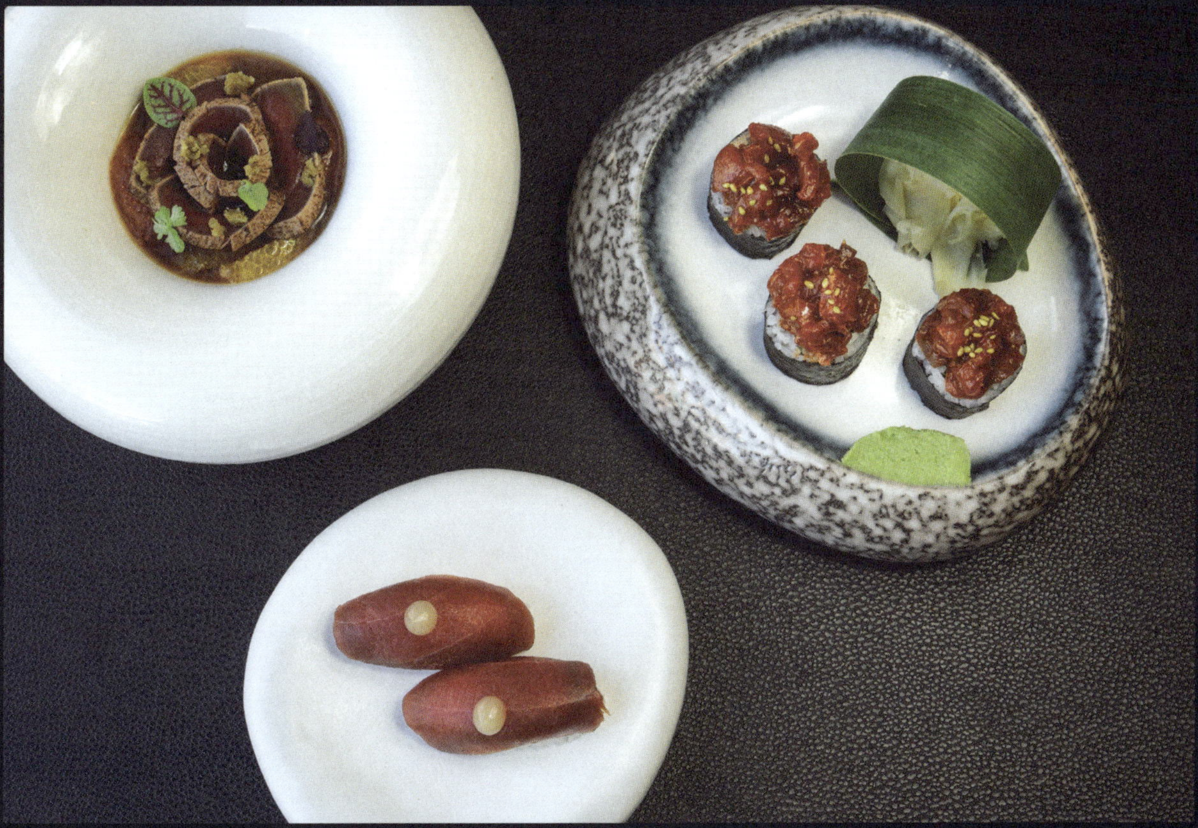

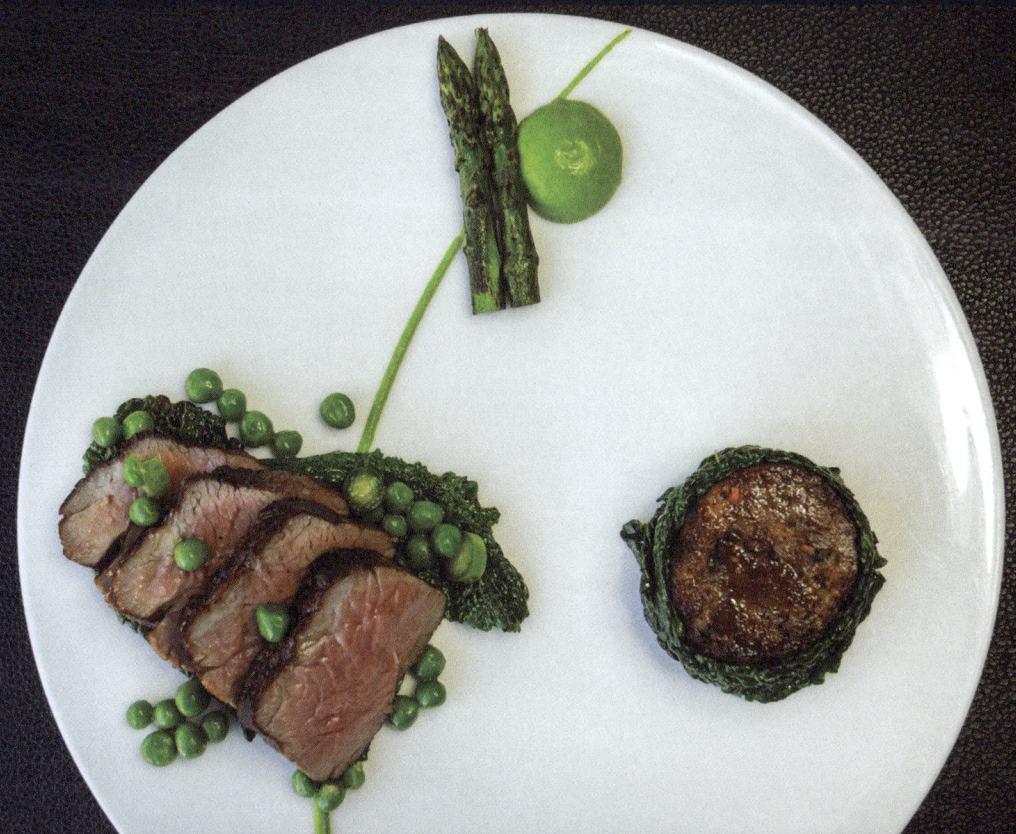

Page 162 Barbequed Irish spring lamb rump, braised lamb shoulder, wasabi and pea puree

Pan-fried monkfish with Thai red curry foam, lemon puree and kohlrabi and celeriac remoulade

Ingredients

Monkfish trimmed – 280g

Thai red curry sauce

Red curry paste - 200g
Garlic - 80g
Fresh chilli - 80g
Lemongrass - 2 stalks
Lime leaves - 4
Galangal - 50g
Water - 50ml
Shallots - 100g
Coconut milk - 800ml
Palm sugar - 50g
Fish sauce - 2 tbsp
Ginger - 50g
Lecithin powder - 5g

Kohl rabi

Kohl rabi - 1
Water - 1l
Ginger - 50g
Rosemary sprig - 1
Lemongrass - 20g
Sugar - 5g
Butter - 5g
Salt - 5g

Lemon purée

Lemon Peel - 250g
Lemon Juice - 250g
Sugar - 50g
Agar agar - 50g
Butter - 80g. Melted
Water - 40ml
Salt - 10g

Celeriac remoulade

Celeriac - 1 medium. 600g
Salt - 30g
Limes - 2
Wasabi paste - 100g
Mayonnaise - 40g
Coriander - 30g
Caster sugar - 10g
Flat parsley - 30g

Method

Serves 4

Monkfish Pre-heat the oven to 200°C. Trim tail by removing the skin and sinew. Cut into 280g pieces and season with salt. Bring the pan to a medium heat and add oil. Once the oil is hot, add the monkfish. Sear on the same side for 2 mins. Reduce to a low heat and sear on the other side for 2 mins. Put the monkfish into the oven for 5 mins (do not turn the monkfish). Remove from oven after the allotted 5 mins and add 2 large knobs of butter. Once the butter has started to foam, begin to baste the monkfish for approx 2 mins. Use a temperature probe whilst continuing to baste until the monkfish has reached 55°C. Rest for 3 mins.

Kohl rabi Peel kohl rabi using a parisienne scoop. Twist into kohl rabi creating small balls (as many as possible). Bring a pan of water to the boil and add 1 lemon peel, 1 slice of fresh ginger, 1 knob of butter, a pinch of salt and a sprig of rosemary. Boil for 1 min. Add kohl rabi balls to the water and blanche for 3 mins. After 3 mins remove the kohl rabi balls and add to ice-cold water. Roast kohl rabi balls in the pre-heated oven for 1 min in preparation for plating.

Celeriac, wasabi and lime remoulade Peel celeriac and finely slice using Japanese mandoline. Finely slice the celeriac and add salt and set aside for 1 hr. Squeeze all the moisture from the celeriac and place into a bowl. Squeeze fresh lime juice and add wasabi, mayonnaise, and coriander. Thoroughly mix in a bowl.

Lemon Purée Peel and juice the lemons – equal quantities. Blanch and refresh the lemon peels 7 times. Blitz lemon juice, lemon peel, water, melted butter and agar together. Slowly add melted butter and pass through a fine sieve.

Thai red curry sauce Finely chop garlic, red chilies, lemongrass, shallots, galangal, palm sugar and lime leaves. Gently cook in oil for 30 mins until soft. Add in red curry paste and sweat for 10 mins. Add coconut milk and cook for a further 45 mins until desired consistency. Remove from heat and allow it to stand for 10 mins and add in fish sauce. Finally pass through a fine sieve, add lecithin powder and blitz with a hand blender to create foam.

For Plating First Add your lemon purée dots however you like. Place your kohl rabi balls (3 per portion) and a generous amount of celeriac, wasabi and lime remoulade. Then place your Monkfish onto the plate and lastly heat up your Thai red curry in a pot. Use a hand blender to create the foam consistency and spoon plenty of sauce around the plate.

Barbequed Irish spring lamb rump, braised lamb shoulder, wasabi and pea puree with lamb jus

Ingredients

Lamb rump

Lamp rump - 280g
Butter milk - 500ml
Gochugaru flakes - 20g
Garlic - 4 cloves
Rosemary - 2 sprigs
Ginger - 20g
Orange peel - 1
Lemongrass - 2 stalks
Green peppercorns - 10g

Lamb shoulder

Cavolo nero - 2 leaves
Gochujang paste - 100g
Coriander seeds - 50g
Garlic - 5 cloves
Shallot - 1 large
Carrots - 2
Lamb shoulder - 1kg
Salt - 300g

Wasabi and pea purée

Wasabi paste - 10g
Shallot - 1
Caster sugar - 10g
Salt - 5g
Butter - 10g
Petite pois peas - 500g
Mint leaves - 2
Water - 200ml

Lamb jus

Shallots - 2
Garlic cloves - 4
Thyme - 1 bunch
Lamb stock - 1l
Butter - 2 tbsp
Sherry vinegar - 1 tbsp
Caster sugar - 2 tbsp

Garnish

Asparagus - 2 stalks
Petit pois peas - 40g
Cavolo Nero - 1 leaf

Method

Serves 4

Lamb rump Pre-heat the oven to 200°C. Trim lamb rump of any sinew or cartilage and score lamb fat. Marinade in butter milk, gochugaru flakes, crushed garlic, rosemary sprigs, lemongrass, orange peel, ginger and green peppercorns for 24 hrs. Brush off marinade and allow it to dry for 1 hr. Cook on a Japanese konro grill using binchotan coals. Wait until the coals are red hot, grill the lamb fat side down first. Move on to each side until sealed, every 1 – 2 mins and continue the process for 10 mins until the lamb is charred on all sides. Place into a pre-heated oven for 6 mins. Remove meat from the oven and probe until 50°C temperature has been reached. Rest for 5 mins and carve.

Lamb Shoulder Cure lamb shoulder in salt for 24 hrs. Rinse off. Add marinade of coriander seeds, gochujang paste and slow cook at 82°C for 8 hrs. Remove from the oven and pass the liquid through a sieve and reduce by 3/4. Pull lamb shoulder. Add reduced lamb stock. Sweat off in a pan finely diced shallots and carrots until soft and mix into the pulled lamb shoulder.

Blanch cavolo nero leaves for 1 min then refresh in ice cold water to stop the cooking process. Spread two layers of clingfilm on a flat surface, place cavolo nero leaves flat on top of cling film. Place lamb shoulder mixture on top of cavolo nero leaves. In a long cylinder shape about the thickness of a rolling pin, fold until the cavolo nero completely covers the mix and roll tight, using both ends as leverage. Pierce clingfilm to remove air bubbles and leave in the fridge for 3 hrs to set. Remove clingfilm and slice 2 cm thick. Roast slices in the oven for 8 mins and serve.

Pea and wasabi purée Sweat shallots in butter on a low heat for 5 mins. Add salt, sugar and wasabi paste. Continue to cook on low heat for 10 mins continuously stirring. Add water and bring to the boil. Add peas and bring back to boil. Add mint leaves and remove from heat. Transfer into a Vitamix or Thermomix. Add butter and blend until smooth. Pass through a fine sieve.

Lamb jus Sweat shallots, garlic and thyme slowly in a pot for 5 mins until the shallots are soft. Add butter and continue to cook gently for a further 5 mins, add in lamb stock, increase heat and reduce by half. Add sherry vinegar and sugar to taste.

To serve In a preferred white plate, heat up your purée and transfer to a small squeezy bottle and add a dot and/or swipe as seen pictured. After the lamb rump has been rested bring back to heat in a pan and carve into four slices. Serve on a bed on extra peas and cavolo nero. Blanch in a pot of salted water for 1 min and char with a blowtorch. Add your lamb shoulder to plate whilst hot, pour lamb jus and serve.

Pistachio crème brulee

Ingredients

Double cream - 1l
Egg yolks - 200g
Caster sugar - 150g
100% pistachio paste - 80g
Pistachio nuts - 30g
Extra sugar for caramelizing brulee

Method

In a pot bring the cream to the boil. Once up to temperature remove from heat and with a spatula combine with the pistachio paste until smooth. In a separate bowl combine egg yolks with sugar without aerating it too much. Now combine the previously mixed yolks with the resulting cream in three turns so as not to cook the egg yolks. Fill terracotta dishes with the resulting mix and bake in a water bath/bain-marie for 35 – 40 minutes at 135°C. Once baked the crème brulee will need to chill overnight in the fridge (minimum 8 hrs). The next day cover crème brulee with a dusting of caster sugar and with a blowtorch caramelize until the sugar has dissolved to a nice crack. Finely chop pistachio nuts roughly and add on top of crème brulee. Enjoy!

19 Bailiú Restaurant
Stephen Holland
Executive head chef

"We focus on fresh, seasonal, organic food sourced locally. We strive to tell our supplier's story on a plate and elevate it."

Bailu restaurant, (Bailu is Scot's Irish for "gathering"), serves modern contemporary Irish food at the exclusive Five-Star Dunluce Resort on Northern Ireland's beautiful Causeway Coast. The restaurant uses the best of ingredients from local suppliers cooked by the finest chefs that matches the expectations of what customers expect from a resort like Dunluce Lodge.

I had a love of cooking from an early age which was inspired by my mother and great aunt, both wonderful cooks, who taught me to appreciate great home cooking and educated me on what good food was. Another woman who greatly inspired me was my college lecturer, Susanne Workman. Through her, I got a position at the world-famous Castle Leslie resort in the Republic of Ireland where I worked under executive head chef Noel McMeel for four-and-a-half lovely years.

After that, I travelled extensively learning about new food, places and culture.

I came back home in 2010 and took up the post of sous chef, then promoted to executive sous chef and finally executive head chef at the Lough Erne Resort before, in 2024 becoming executive head chef at Dunluce Lodge to oversee all the culinary operations Dunluce lodge offers.

One of the highlights at Bailu is a fabulous Lough Neagh eel, perfectly smoked, and paired with homemade dashi stock, accompanied by a beautiful Kilkeel seared scallop. A simple dish but very effective and full of big flavours. We also offer fantastic plumbridge venison supplied by Lisdergan Meats owned by Ian McKernaghan, one of Ireland's best butchers. We marinate the venison in a traditional base of garlic, thyme and aromatics, served with a robust red wine gel and sour white cabbage, to create a spectacular dish full of flavour.

We focus on fresh, seasonal, organic food sourced locally. We strive to tell our supplier's story on a plate and elevate it.

One of the biggest challenges of my career was when I was executive sous chef at Lough Erne when the resort hosted the G8 world summit in 2013. The security was ferocious. World leaders such as President Obama, Prime Minister Cameron and Russian leader Putin were attending and the logistical exercise to get the food into the resort past the intense security into the kitchen was immense. We had to think on our feet and overcome the obstacles, but we succeeded. That's one of the things about being a good chef, you need to adapt to different circumstances and surmount them.

I am a keen advocate for my chefs to be creative with their suggestions to generate new dishes. Its important chefs feel they're being listened to because you're encouraging their creativity and generating a learning environment. A team of chefs singing from the same hymn sheet produces a great atmosphere and amazing food.

The people are what make Northern Ireland and Dunluce Lodge tick. The team commit their time and devotion into making Bailu an amazing restaurant, creating a unique experience for our guests.

Toomebridge smoked eel

Ingredients

Toomebridge smoked eel - 200g

Apple - 40g

Yellow beetroot - 40g

Burren balsamic pearls - 20g

Black apple butter - 20ml

Trout roe - 10g

Caviar - 5g

Cucumber - 10g

Dill - 2g

Mussenden sea salt - 1g

Method

Serves 4

Remove the fat from the belly of the eel, and cut into even slices. Dice the beetroot in even cubes. Peel the cucumber and cut length ways. Remove the seeds and cut into even dices.

To assemble the dish Add the black butter to a piping bag and neatly add 9 dots. Individually dot on top of the eel. With a Small spoon add caviar to your liking. Make sure it is even and not touching any other ingredients.

Similar to the Caviar, add an even amount of roe to the eel. I generally use the trout roe as the main garnish for this dish as its colour is pronounced and vibrant, so please place centrally.

Add the diced cucumber to the top of the eel, again making sure it is not in contact with any other ingredient. Gently add the dill to finish the garnishing. Sprinkle with Mussenden Sea Salt to finish.

< Toomebridge smoked eel

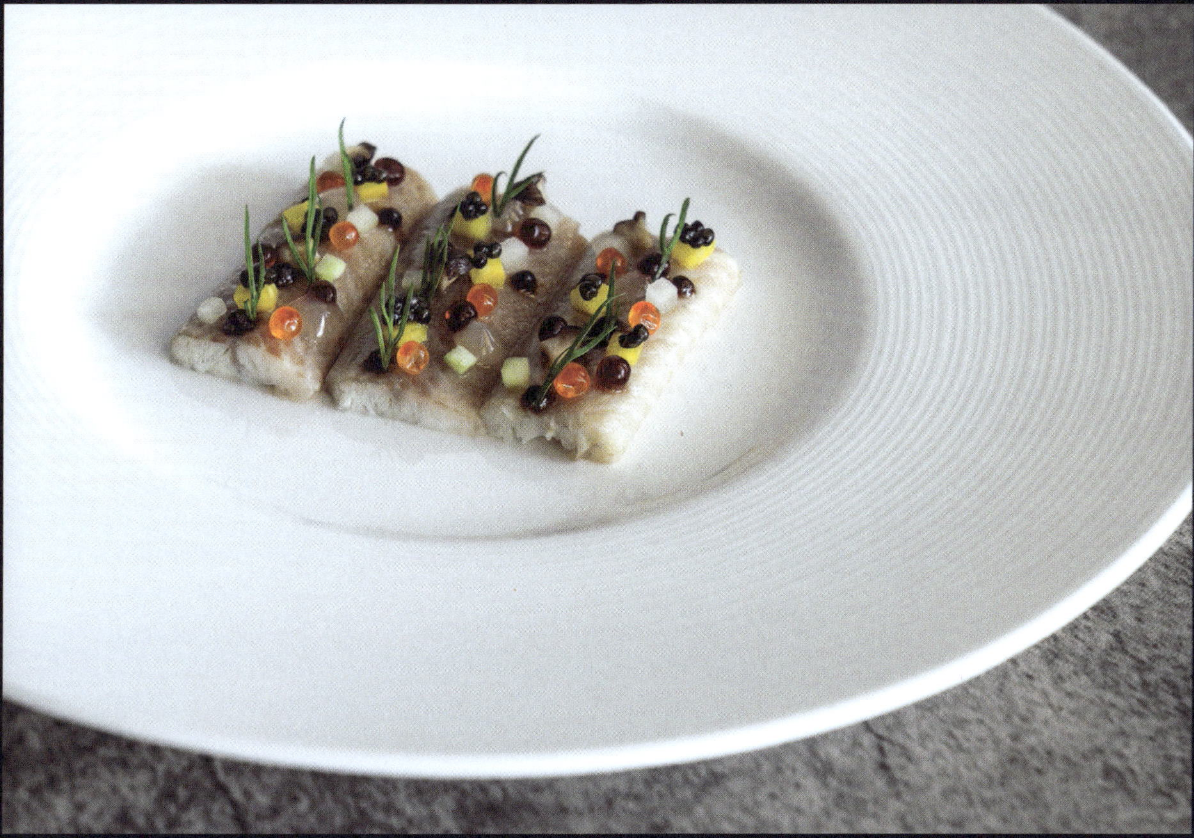

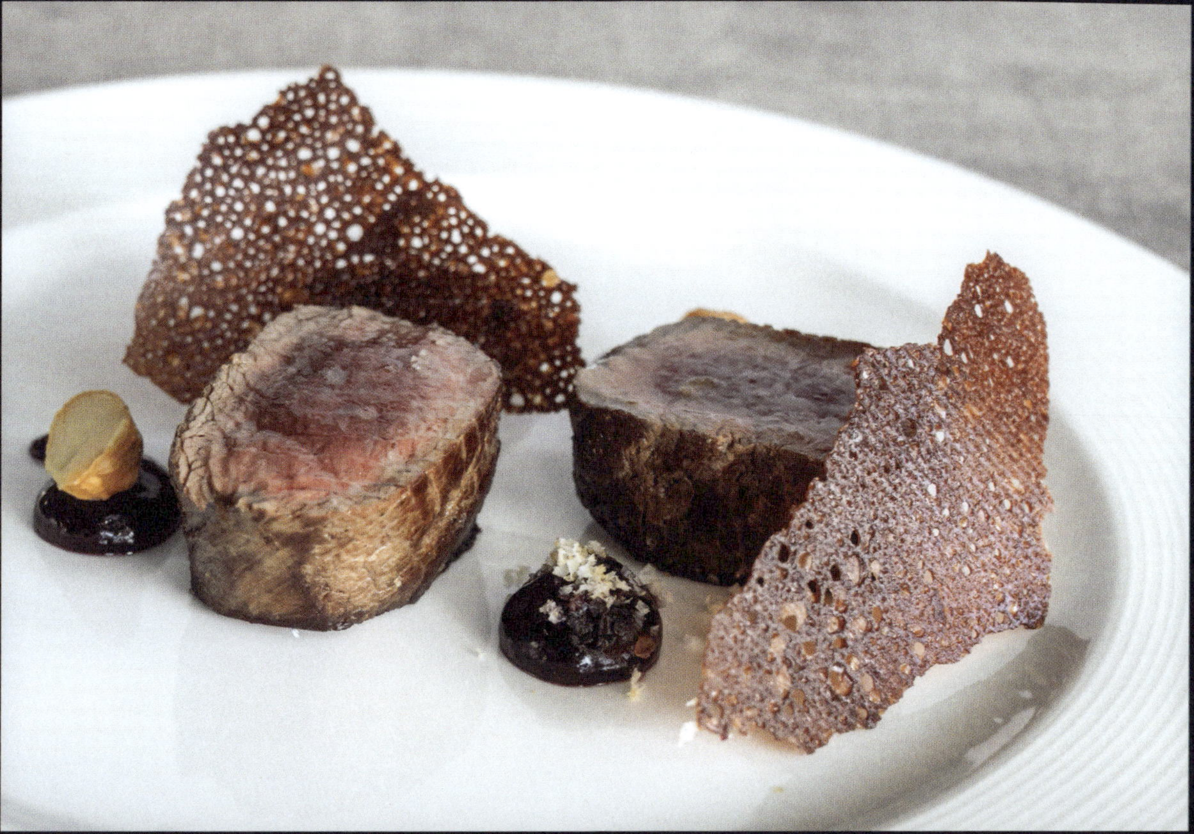

Page 170 Plumbridge venison

Kilkeel scallops

Ingredients

Scallops

Scallops - 4

Salt - 1g

Butter - 5g

Vegetable oil

Wild garlic emulsion

Wild garlic - 100g. Washed

Cidre vinegar - 50ml

Egg - 50g

Garlic - 20g

Salt - 2g

Djon mustard - 5g

Vegetable oil - 200ml

Lovage oil

Lovage - 100g

Vegetable oil - 100ml

White wine cream

Cream - 100ml

White wine - 50ml

Bay leaf - 2g

Thyme - 2g

Garlic - 5g

Celery - 5g

Shallot - 10g

Salt - 2g

Pepper - 2g

Method

Serves 4

Scallops Remove the roe from the scallop and place on a clean tray ready to cook.

Wild garlic emulsion Wash the wild garlic leaves. In a blender use 200ml of oil and blend with the wild garlic leaves until you create a wild garlic oil. Strain the mix through a fine sieve to remove any pulp so you have a clear green liquid. Set aside to make the emulsion.

In a blender add the egg, garlic and mustard, then slowly add the oil to make the emulsion. Add the cider vinegar to season with some salt. Add to a piping bag and pipe into a squeezy bottle.

Lovage oil Same principle for the wild garlic oil. Wash the leaves and add the oil and leaves to the blender and blend until the leaves make a vibrant green oil. Pass through a fine sieve to remove the pulp and add to a squeezy bottle.

White wine cream sauce Add the diced shallot, diced celery, garlic, thyme, bay leaf to a pot and lightly sauté until the shallot and celery are cooked. Add the white wine and reduce by half. Then add the cream and reduce by half until it coats the back of a spoon. Pass through a sieve and season to taste with salt and pepper.

To plate Lightly season the scallops and sear them in a hot pan. Glaze the scallops with the butter to achieve a golden brown colour on each side. Remove and rest for 1 min.

For the lovage Heat the white wine cream, but do not boil. Gently add the lovage oil but do not mix the sauce. The sauce should have the appearance of a split sauce. Add the dots of the wild garlic emulsion to the plate. Add the sauce to cover the base of the plate.

To finish Add the scallop to the center of the plate and garnish with apple matchsticks.

< Kilkeel scallops

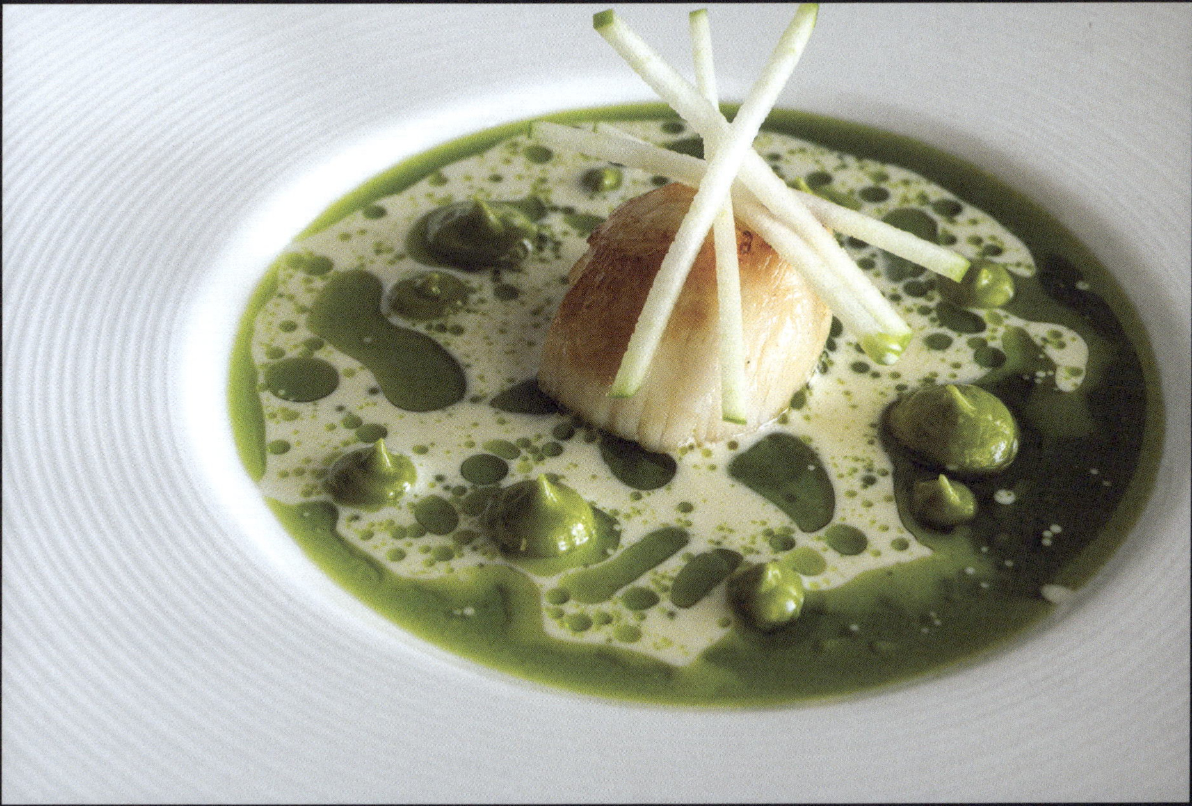

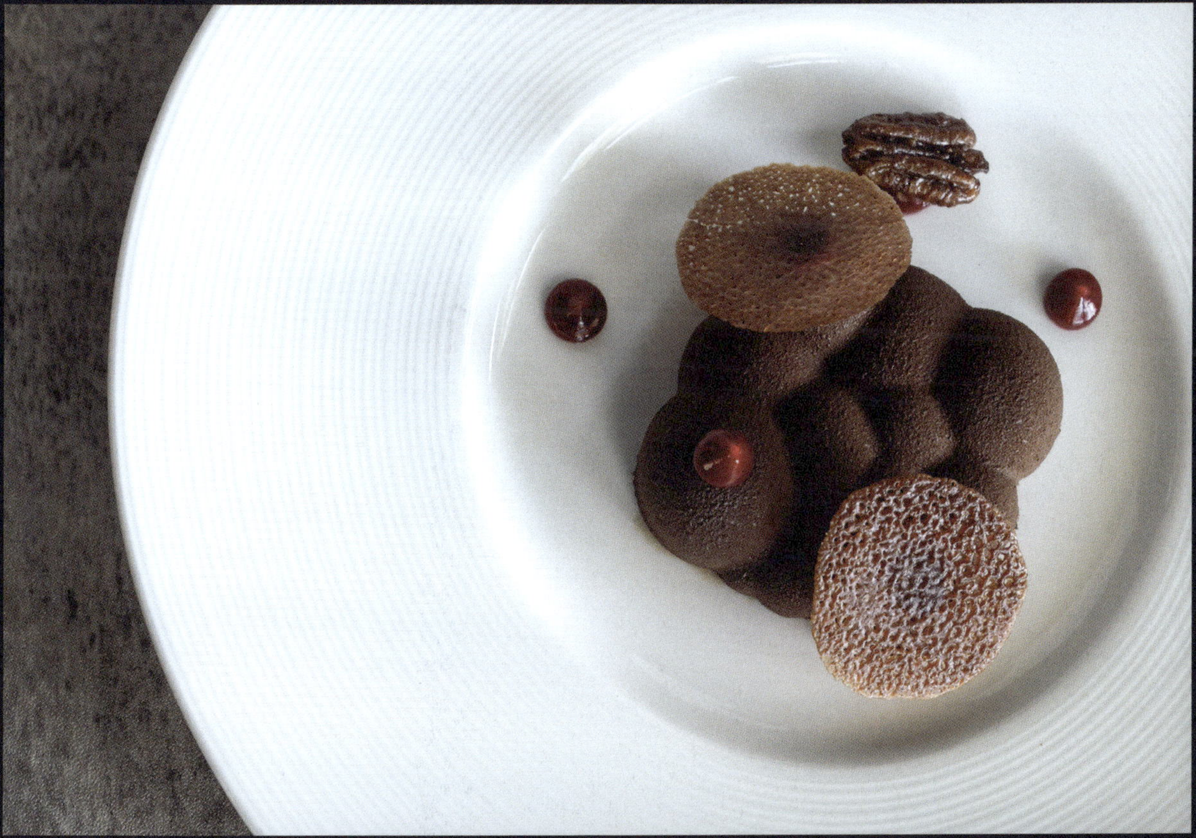

Page 171 Chocolate delice

Plumbridge venison

Ingredients

Venison striploin

Venison - 200g
Thyme - 500ml
Garlic - 40g
Vegetable oil

Red wine gel

Red wine - 100ml
Agar agar - 1g
Sugar - 50g
Bay leaf - 3g
Thyme - 3g

Pickle white cabbage

White cabbage - 200g
Burren balsamic - 100ml sheets
Green peppercorns - 5g
Bay leaf - 3g. Optional

Candied macadamia nut

Macadamia nut - 500g
Sugar - 50g
Sea salt - 50g

Red Wine Jus

Venison bones - 200g
Veal stock - 200ml
Thyme - 5g
Garlic - 5g
Celery - 15g
Carrot - 15g
Shallot - 30g
Bay leaf - 5g
Red wine - 100ml
Salt - 5g
Pepper - 5g

Cocca nib tuile

Cocao nibs - 10g
Butter - 75g
Sugar - 180g
Cocoa powder - 15g
Plain Flour - 30g
Cherry vinegar - 90ml

Method

Venison To remove the loin from the saddle, carefully remove the meat from the bone by running the knife down the backbone and along the rib section until all meat has being removed. Remove all fat and sinew. Marinate the prepped venison loin in garlic, rosemary and thyme. Roll in cling film to achieve a tight cylinder effect – perfect for cutting a 200g portion.

Red wine gel Add red wine, sugar, bay leaf and thyme to the pot. Gently bring to the boil and add the agar agar. Bring to the boil and strain the herbs from the liquid. Place the liquid in large container so it will cool quickly and set. Once set add the jelly to a blender and blend to smooth consistency.

Pickled cabbage Finely slice the cabbage in julienne strips. This takes time, but the cooking process greatly quickens and you are left with a better result. Add all the ingredients into a pot and cook until the cabbage is nicely cooked and slightly caramelized. The liquid in the pot should be a sweet glaze by this stage. Keep the cabbage in this glaze to achieve a high gloss finish.

Candied macadamia nut Cook the nuts with the sugar and water for 40 mins. Remove and bake in the oven until golden brown, season with rock salt and allow to cool.

Red wine jus Roast the venison saddle after preparing the loins. Large dice the root vegetables and add to large pot and sweat off until golden brown. Add the bones and red wine. Reduce the red wine by half and add the veal stock. Do not boil, but simmer and remove any excess fat from the stock by skimming the top. Strain the mix and reduce to a consistency that coats the back of the spoon. Season to taste. If you find the jus is slightly bitter, use some cherry vinegar and sugar. Mix well together and season until the bitter taste is neutralised. Strain again through a fine sieve. Set aside with cling film over the pot to stop a skin forming on the top of the jus.

Tuile Cream together your butter and sugar, add cherry vinegar, flour and cocoa powder together until smooth, spread flat on silicone mat and sprinkle some cocoa nibs over the mix and bake at 170°C for 7 mins. Use a cutter or knife to create your desired shape.

To plate Sear the venison loin (200g) portion until caramelized on all sides, place in the oven at 180°C for 5 mins and rest, you are looking for a nice med-rare center.

Quenelle the cabbage and add the red wine gel to the plate. Cut the macadamia nuts in half and place on top of the red wine gel. Slice the venison in half and let to rest. Make sure all excess blood is gone before adding to the plate, finely add the tuile to garnish and serve the jus in a side jug.

Chocolate delice

Ingredients

Dark chocolate delice

Castor sugar - 400g

Eggs - 5

Egg yolks - 170g

Dark chocolate 72% (melted) - 900g

Cream - 1250g

Chocolate malt spray

Cocca butter - 4. 200 – 400g each

Dark chocolate - 500ml

Raspberry gel

Raspberry puree - 500ml

Agar agar - 500ml

Sugar - 200ml

Tuile

Butter - 75g

Sugar - 180g

Cocoa powder - 15g

Plain flour - 30g

Cherry vinegar - 90ml

Method

Serves 4

Delice Cream your sugar and eggs together. Add the chocolate until smooth. Whip the cream and add to the chocolate mix. Pour into the mould and freeze. To De Mould, make sure the mix is solid and completely frozen. Place on a tray to add to the freezer again until ready to spray.

Tuile Cream together your butter and sugar. Add cherry vinegar, flour and cocoa powder together until smooth. Spread flat on silicone mat and bake at 170°C for 7 mins. Use a cutter or knife to create your desired shape.

Raspberry gel Gently bring the raspberry purée and the sugar to the boil. Add the agar agar and whisk to remove any lumps. Bring to the boil again and remove to a large container to cool and set. Once set add to a blender and blend until smooth. Add to a piping bag and fill a squeezy bottle for plating.

Cocca butter spray Melt the cocoa butter and add the dark chocolate until mix is smooth. Once cooled to 33°C, add mix to spray gun tank and begin to spray the delice. Make sure not to go too close to the delice. The effect on the delice should have a matted reflection. Store in fridge until ready to serve.

To serve Once the delice is sprayed, place in the center of the plate and add the Tuile garnish and add gel on the plate for garnish.

20 Lir
Stevie and Rebekah McCarry
Head chef & co-owners

Situated on the north coast of Northern Ireland, Lir offers wonderful delights from Ireland's rich seafood larder. With a menu that changes daily depending on the catch brought in from local boats, Lir provides sustainable and delicious seafood to the local community and tourists alike.

Rebekah and Stevie's vision was always to own their own restaurant. After years of searching, in early 2020 they found premises at a former yacht club in Coleraine marina. But, almost immediately, covid struck. Needing to adapt, they opened as a fishmonger as there were very few places locally where fish was available.

Working with the fishing community across the north coast and Donegal, the couple bought 25 lobsters from a local boat 'Boy Matthew' and advertised on Instagram resulting in an instant sell out. The following week more white fish were collected off the boats in Donegal, brought back to Lir and delivered door to door.

Aware that hospitality is a transient industry they used market research to build up a strong customer base. They opened the restaurant after lockdown reckoning that people who bought fish at the shop would be likely to eat there. It worked. The community has supported the venture, and Lir has received great reviews including a fantastic one from the Guardian food critic, Jay Raynor, who paid a surprise visit.

Lir is a one-stop shop where people can buy fish over the counter on a Tuesday and come to the restaurant for the tasting menu or choose a combination of small and big plates where customers can order as much as they want.

Head chef Stevie is passionate about making seafood approachable with an innovative menu that includes a monkfish and coley sausage roll with cross-laminated pastry, or squid Bolognese and cod collar schnitzel with brandy and mushroom sauce. Not forgetting such delights as smoked dogfish corndog or Turkish style fish koftas. It's not all about haddock and chips!

Lir source their supplies from local providers such as Rhee River Organics or forage in nearby forests or along the coastal path for three cornered leek, wood sorrel and herbs such as primrose and gorse which is used for garnish, cocktails, desserts and sauces.

Rebekah and Stevie are focused on minimizing waste. There is a Clear Bin policy in the kitchen. As Stevie says, "if more people checked their bins, they'd realise the profits they're wasting." At Lir, recycling is everything. Bones are used as stock. Skins are dehydrated and used as crackling while fish organs are fermented and used as flavoursome sauces like the mackerel garum. At Lir, sustainability and zero waste are vital to make the business viable.

Stevie won the regional Northern Ireland heat of Great British Menu in 2025 which has earned Lir further great publicity, alongside winning Best Chef, Best Restaurant & Best sustainable practices in Derry at the Restaurant Association of Ireland awards 2025.

People in Northern Ireland have become much more appreciative of food with higher expectations which leads to higher standards and better quality. Lir is certainly making a vital contribution to that thriving dining scene.

"Lir offers wonderful delights from Ireland's rich seafood larder."

Stevie McCarry, head chef and co-owner

Lobster "all ways"
Lobster head and tail, lobster bisque, lobster head oil and lobster head mayo on Vittle bakeshop brioche

Ingredients

Lobster

Lobsters - 2 live. Approx. 500 – 600g each

Sea salt

Ice water

Lobster bisque

Shells and heads from 2 lobsters

Olive oil - 1 tbsp

Onion - 1. Finely chopped

Carrots - 2 small. Chopped

Celery - 1 stick. Chopped

Garlic - 2 cloves. Crushed

Tomato purée - 1 1/2 tbsp

Dry white wine - 125ml

Brandy - 1 tbsp

Fish or shellfish stock - 800ml

Double cream - 100ml

Bay leaf - 1 sprig

Thyme - 1 sprig

A few parsley stalks (bouquet garni)

Lobster oil

Reserved cooked lobster heads

Neutral oil - 150ml. Rapeseed or sunflower etc.

Garlic - 1 clove. Crushed

Thyme - 1 sprig

Orange - 1/2. Zest

Lobster mayo

Egg yolk - 1

Dijon mustard - 1 tsp

Lemon juice - 2 tsp

Lobster oil - 100ml

Salt - To taste

For assembly

Brioche loaf - 2 thick slices. Cut into 4

Butter - For toasting

Cooked lobster tail - Thinly sliced

Micro herbs or chervil (optional)

Lemon segment - To season

Method

Serves 4

This dish epitomises my zero waste ethos as the entirety of the lobster is used. This can be a real show stopper with the bisque poured table side and paired with a white burgundy or champagne.

Lobster Bring a large pot of salted water to a rolling boil. Kill the lobsters humanely, then cook in boiling water for 5 mins. Transfer immediately to ice water. When cooled, remove tails and claws. Extract the meat and reserve the shells and heads.

Lobster bisque In a heavy pan, heat olive oil and add the lobster shells and heads. Cook until red and aromatic. Add chopped onion, carrot, celery, and garlic. Sauté until golden and softened (10 – 12 mins). Stir in tomato purée and cook for 1 – 2 mins. Deglaze with wine and brandy. Reduce slightly. Add stock and bouquet garni. Simmer uncovered for 45 mins. Then strain through a fine sieve. Return liquid to the pan. Add cream, and simmer for 5 – 10 mins. Season with salt.

Lobster oil Heat the oil gently with lobster heads, garlic, thyme, and orange zest for 25 – 30 mins on low heat. Strain and cool completely.

Lobster mayo In a bowl, whisk egg yolk, mustard, and lemon juice until smooth. Slowly add the lobster oil in a thin stream, whisking continuously to emulsify. Season with salt. Chill until needed.

Brioche Lightly butter the brioche. Toast in a dry pan or under a grill until golden and crisp.

To Serve Gently warm sliced lobster tail in a little butter or lobster oil. Pour a shallow pool of bisque into each starter plate or bowl. Add toasted brioche to each dish, topped with lobster slices and a dollop of lobster mayo. Drizzle with lobster oil, and garnish with herbs and a squeeze of lemon.

< Lobster "all ways"

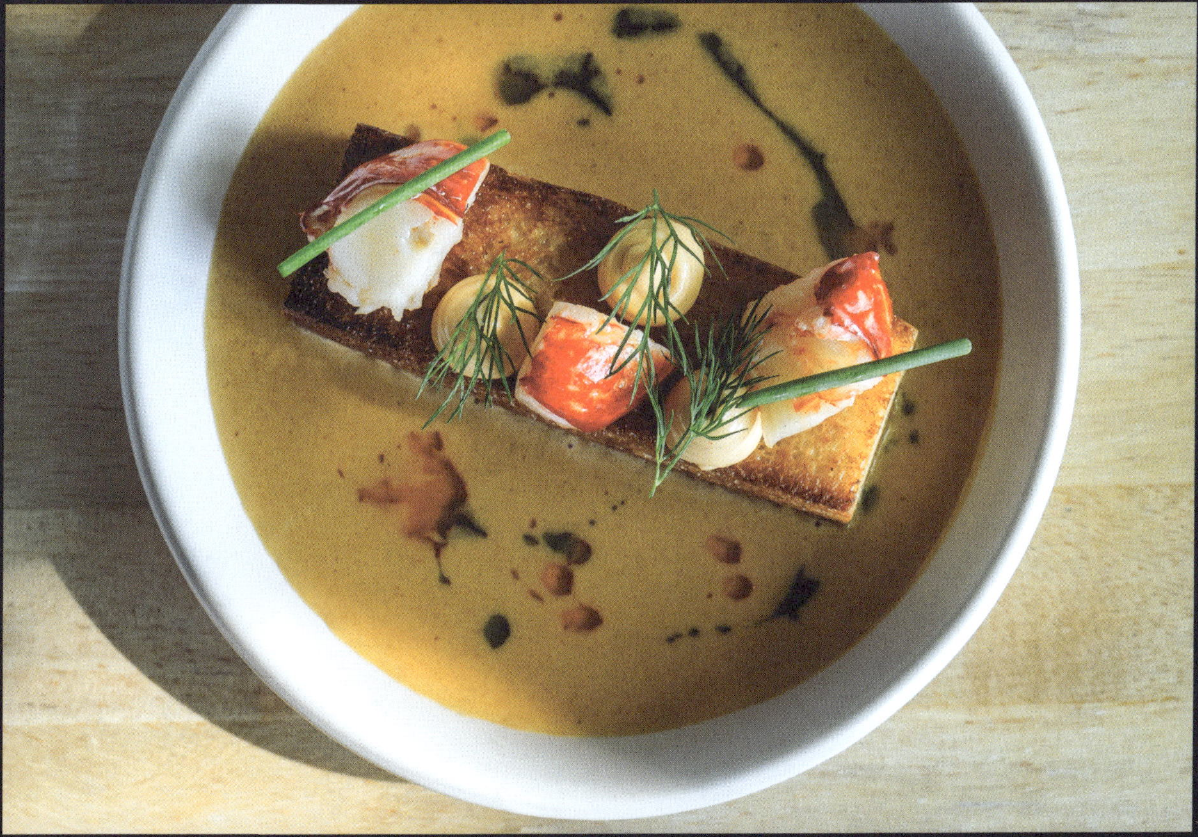

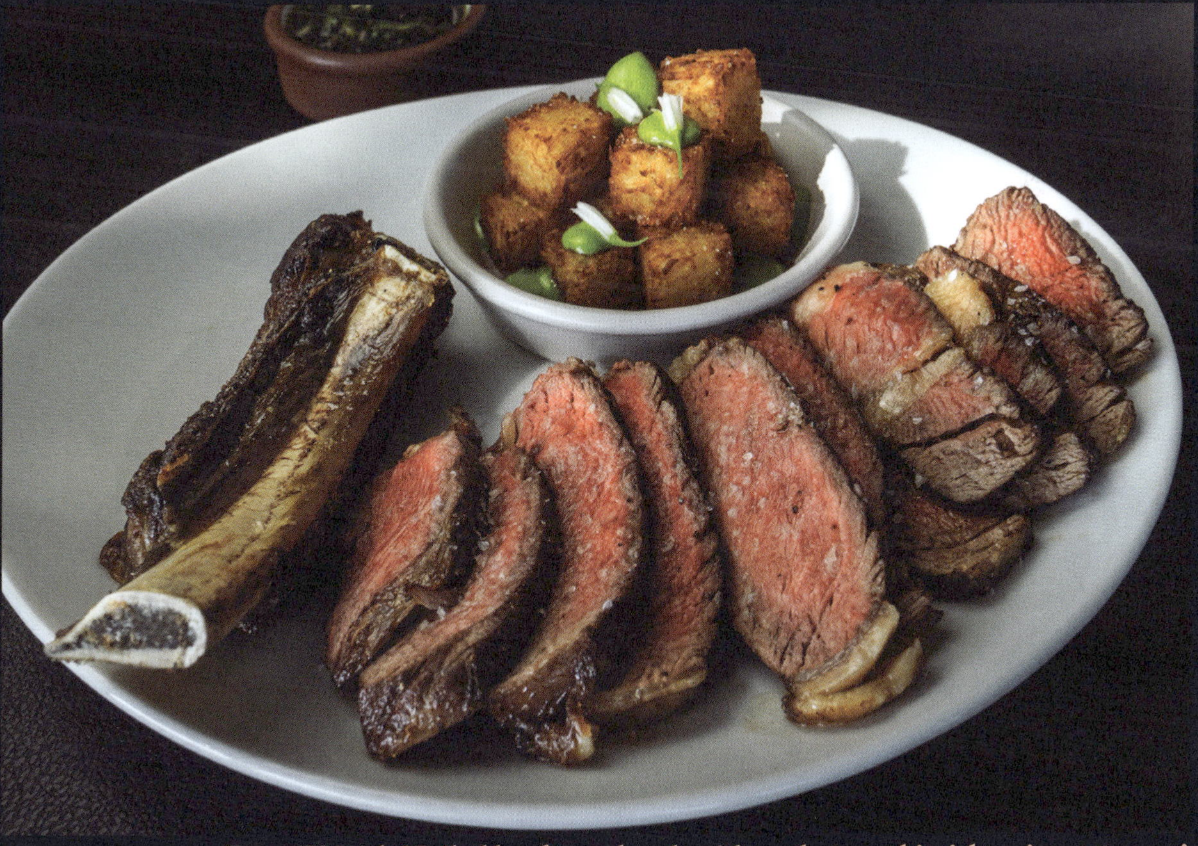

Page 178 Irish Moiled beef tomahawk with sea lettuce chimichurri, potato rosti

Hake Kyiv with wild garlic butter and roasted cauliflower purée

Ingredients

Hake Kyiv

Hake fillets - 4. Approx. 140 – 160g each. Skinless and boneless. Butterflied into 4 long thin portions

Sea salt

Plain flour - 100g

Eggs - 2. Beaten

Panko breadcrumbs - 150g

Neutral oil (e.g. sunflower or rapeseed) - For shallow frying

Transglutaminase powder (e.g. Activa RM) - 4g approx.

Wild garlic butter

Unsalted butter - 100g. Softened

Wild garlic - 30 – 40g. Finely chopped

Lemon - 1/2. Zest

Lemon juice - 1 tsp

Sea salt - A pinch

Nutritional yeast - 1 tsp

Roasted cauliflower purée

Cauliflower - 1 medium. Cut into florets

Olive oil - 2 tbsp

Salt

White pepper

Double cream - 150ml

Unsalted butter - 45g

Optional garnish

Onion seeds

Wild garlic leaves or flowers

Method

Serves 4

This is one of my favourite recipes as it offers a refined fish-based take on the iconic chicken Kyiv and the butter filling can be adapted to suit the season or the guests personal taste. I prefer to use transglutaminase to ensure a perfect seal with no leakage.

Wild garlic butter Combine softened butter, chopped wild garlic, lemon zest, juice, salt and nutritional yeast in a bowl. Roll into a tight log using cling film or baking parchment. Chill until firm, then cut into 4 even pieces.

Form the hake Kyiv Lay out the 4 long thin hake slices and season lightly with salt and white pepper. Place a portion of the garlic butter in the centre of one piece. Lightly dust the inner surfaces along the edge with transglutaminase powder (use approx. 0.5g per Kyiv). Fold one end of the hake over the top to enclose the butter. Shape the fillets into neat cylinders or domes and wrap tightly in cling film. Refrigerate for 6 – 8 hrs (or overnight) to allow the enzyme to bond the fillets together.

Crumb and cook the hake Kyiv Unwrap the set Kyiv fillets. Dredge in flour, then dip in beaten egg and coat in panko breadcrumbs. For added crunch, repeat the egg and crumb step. Chill for 10 – 15 mins to firm. Shallow-fry in hot neutral oil for 3 – 4 mins per side until golden and crisp. Transfer to a preheated 180°C oven for 5 – 6 mins to finish cooking and melt the butter core.

Roasted cauliflower purée Preheat oven to 200°C (180°C fan). Toss cauliflower florets in olive oil, season with salt and roast for 25 – 30 mins until golden. Blend the roasted cauliflower with cream and butter until silky smooth. Adjust seasoning and keep warm until serving.

To serve Spoon a generous dollop or swoosh of cauliflower purée onto each plate. Place the crisp hake Kyiv just off-centre. Garnish with onion seeds, dill or wild garlic leaves and flowers.

< Hake Kyiv with wild garlic butter and roasted cauliflower purée

Page 179 Hawthorn leaf and flower panna cotta with rhubarb gel and fermented rhubarb

Irish Moiled beef tomahawk with sea lettuce chimichurri, potato rosti and wild garlic emulsion

Ingredients

Tomahawks

Irish Moiled beef tomahawk steaks - 2 x 1.2kg. Bone-in

Sea salt and freshly cracked black pepper

Neutral oil (e.g. rapeseed) - For searing

Garlic - 4 cloves. Crushed

Rosemary - 4 sprigs

Unsalted butter - 60g

Sea lettuce chimichurri

4 tbsp dried sea lettuce (or 20g fresh) - 4 tbsp. Finely chopped

Banana shallot - 1. Finely diced

Garlic - 2 cloves. Finely grated

Sherry vinegar - 3 tbsp

Lemon - 1. Zest

Capers - 2 tsp. Chopped

Chilli flakes - 1 tsp. Optional

Parsley - 4 tbsp. Chopped

Coriander or mint - 2 tbsp. Chopped

Extra virgin olive oil - 150ml

Sea salt - To taste

Potato rosti

Floury potatoes - 4 large. e.g. Maris Piper

Banana shallot - 1. Grated. Optional

Duck fat or unsalted butter - 2 tbsp

Salt and white pepper

Neutral oil - For shallow frying

Wild garlic emulsion

Egg yolks - 2

Dijon mustard - 2 tsp

Lemon juice - 2 tbsp

Wild garlic oil - 140ml. See method

Sea salt - To taste

Method

Serves 4

The two tomahawks provide plenty of meat for four as a main course and provide a show-stopping presentation.

Tomahawks Bring the tomahawks to room temperature for at least 1 hr. Season all sides generously with salt and pepper. Preheat the oven to 160°C (fan). Sear each tomahawk individually in a hot, heavy skillet for 3 – 4 mins per side, including edges, until a deep crust forms. Add garlic, rosemary and butter to each pan while searing, and baste for 1 – 2 mins. Transfer both tomahawks to a wire-racked tray. Roast for 18 mins at 155°C, or until the internal temperature reads 50 – 52°C (medium-rare). Rest under foil for 15 mins before carving.

Sea lettuce chimichurri If using dried sea lettuce, rehydrate in warm water for 5 mins. Drain and chop finely. Mix with shallot, garlic, vinegar, lemon zest, capers, chilli flakes, and chopped herbs. Stir in olive oil and season with salt. Let sit for 15 – 30 mins to infuse.

Make the potato rosti Peel and coarsely grate the potatoes. Squeeze out all excess moisture with a clean towel. Mix with shallot, duck fat/butter, salt, and white pepper. Divide into 16 equal cubes. Shallow-fry in neutral oil over medium heat for 3 – 4 mins per side until crisp and golden. Finish in the oven at 180°C for 2.5 – 5 mins, checking regularly, to ensure they're cooked through.

Wild garlic emulsion First of all make the wild garlic oil by blending 80g wild garlic with 160ml neutral oil, heat gently to 70°C, then cool and strain. In a bowl, whisk yolks, mustard and lemon juice until smooth. Slowly drizzle in wild garlic oil while whisking until emulsified. Season with salt and chill.

To serve Slice the rested tomahawks into thick pieces, across the grain. Cut up crispy rosti into bite-size pieces place in dish and garnish with wild garlic emulsion and wild garlic flowers. Top or flank with generous slices of steak. Spoon chimichurri over and around the meat.

Chef's notes The two tomahawks provide plenty of meat for four as a main course – expect a show-stopping presentation. You can cook and hold the rosti warm in the oven while carving the beef. Leftover chimichurri is excellent with seafood or eggs.

Hawthorn leaf and flower panna cotta with rhubarb gel and fermented rhubarb

Ingredients

Hawthorn leaf & flower panna cotta

Double cream - 500ml

Whole milk - 200ml

Caster sugar - 80g

Bronze gelatine leaves - 3. Or 6g powdered gelatine

Fresh hawthorn leaves and blossom - 2 generous handfuls. Approx. 20 – 25g loosely packed

Lemon - 1/2 . Zest

Elderflower cordial - 1/2 tsp. Or a few drops hawthorn flower essence for subtle lift. Optional

Rhubarb gel

Rhubarb - 200g. Chopped

Caster sugar - 60g

Water - 50ml

Agar agar powder - 2g

Lemon juice - 1/2 tsp

Fermented rhubarb garnish

Rhubarb stalk - 1. Approx. 150g. Cut into thin batons

Caster sugar - 10g

Filtered water - 150ml

Fine sea salt - 1.5g. 1% by rhubarb weight

Optional - Pink peppercorns, ginger, or a bay leaf

Method

Serves 6

Panna cottas provide a blank canvas for flavour which is why it can be ideal to use with various foraged ingredients throughout the season. For this one I have chosen hawthorn but this recipe can be used with elderflower and meadowsweet using the same quantities.

Hawthorn leaf and flower panna cotta Gently rinse the hawthorn leaves and flowers to remove any insects or dust. In a saucepan, combine the cream and milk. Heat gently until just steaming (not boiling). Add the hawthorn leaves and flowers, remove from heat. Cover and infuse for 30 – 40 mins. Strain through a fine sieve or muslin, pressing gently to extract flavour. Return to pan and stir in the sugar. Soften the gelatine leaves in cold water for 5 mins (or bloom powdered gelatine in 2 tbsp water). Reheat the infused cream to just below a simmer, then remove from heat and whisk in the gelatine until dissolved. Add lemon zest and optional elderflower cordial or hawthorn essence if using. Pour into moulds or ramekins. Chill until set – at least 4 – 6 hrs.

Rhubarb Gel Combine rhubarb, sugar, and water in a pan. Simmer gently for 10 – 15 mins until softened. Blend and strain to get a smooth juice/purée (approx. 180ml). Return to pan, add agar agar, bring to a boil, and simmer for 1 min. Pour into a shallow tray. Once set, blend into a smooth gel. Add lemon juice to brighten, if needed.

Fermented Rhubarb Dissolve salt and sugar in the water to create a light brine. Place rhubarb batons in a clean jar. Add aromatics if desired. Cover with brine and weigh down with a fermentation weight or small bag of brine. Ferment at room temperature for 5 – 7 days, tasting daily for desired tang. Once fermented, store in the fridge in its liquid.

To serve Unmould or plate the panna cotta in chilled bowls or flat plates. Dot or swipe rhubarb gel around or underneath. Garnish with curls or batons of fermented rhubarb. Finish with fresh hawthorn flowers and leaves.

Restaurant details

Artis
29-31 Craft Village,
Londonderry, BT48 6AR.
028 7126 1212

www.artisatcraftvillagederry.com

Bailu Restaurant
Dunluce Lodge, Dunluce Road,
Portrush, BT56 8NB.
028 7053 1700

www.dunlucelodge.com

Culloden Estate and Spa
Bangor Road, Holywood,
Belfast, BT18 0EX
028 9042 1066

www.cullodenestateandspa.com

Cyprus Avenue
228 Upper Newtownards Road,
Belfast, BT4 3ET.
028 9065 6755

www.cyprusavenue.co.uk

Edo
3 Capital House, Unit 2 Upper
Queen Street, Belfast, BT1 6FB.
028 9031 3054

www.edorestaurant.co.uk

Finn Lough Hotel
33 Letter Road, Aghnablaney,
Enniskillen, BT93 2BB.
056 0367 2229

www.finnlough.com

Gillies Grill
Galgorm Resort, 136 Fenaghy
Road, Ballymena, BT42 1EA.
028 2588 1001

www.galgorm.com

Grand Central
9-15 Bedford Street, Belfast,
BT2 7FF.
028 9023 1066

www.grandcentralhotelbelfast.com

La Bottega
625 LisburnRoad, Belfast,
BT9 7GT.
028 9049 0340

www.labottegabelfast.co.uk

Lir
Marina, Lir, 66 Portstewart
Road, Coleraine, BT52 1EY.
07828127739

www.lirseafood.com

Lo & Slo

12 Sicily Park, Londonderry,
BT47 5QP.

028 7116 6277

www.lo-slo.co.uk

Lough Erne Resort

Belleek Road, Enniskillen,
BT93 7ED.

028 6632 3230

www.lougherneresort.com

No 14 at the Georgian House

14 The Square, Comber,
Newtownards, BT23 5DT.

028 9131 1106

www.no14georgianhouse.com

The Ebrington

Ebrington Square, Derry,
BT47 6FA.

028 7122 0700

www.theebringtonhotel.com

The Old Inn

15-25 Main Street, Crawfordsburn,
Bangor, BT19 1JH.

028 9185 3255

www.theoldinn.com

The Street Kitchen

30 Paget Lane, Enniskillen,
BT74 7HT.

07711871156

www.thestreetkitchenenniskillen.com

The Tailor's House

50 Main Street, Ballygawley,
Dungannon, BT70 2HE.

028 8556 8910

www.thetailorshouse.co.uk

Tully Mill

Florencecourt, Enniskillen,
BT92 1FN.

028 6634 9879

www.tullymill.com

28 at the Hollow

6 Church Street, Enniskillen,
BT74 7EJ.

028 6632 8224

www.28atthehollow.com

UMI

57 Strand Road, Londonderry,
BT48 7NW.

028 7187 8399

www.umiderry.co.uk

Recipe index

Ferrier Richardson

Ferrier Richardson is one of Scotland's finest and best-known chefs. He has travelled the world extensively, representing Scotland for multi-national companies and government departments.

Earlier in his career he was responsible for re-establishing the culinary reputation of The Rogano and The Buttery, he was the opening Executive Chef for Glasgow's first Five Star Hotel and has owned several multi award winning restaurants that have featured in all the major guidebooks.

He is a Gold Medallist at The Culinary Olympics, Food Asia, Team manager of the award winning Scottish and British Culinary Olympic teams and was crowned Scotland's Master Chef of The Year.

Currently he owns the multi award winning Gastro Pub, The East End Fox based in the east end of Glasgow and the Auldhouse Arms in East Kilbride, that specialise in elevated comfort food.

Over and above this, he works privately worldwide and has a client list that includes Royalty, Presidents, A list celebrities, world class international sport stars and extremely high net worth individuals.

He prides himself on the quality of his food, professionalism and the privacy of his clients.

His food philosophy is to source the best ingredients and allow them to speak for themselves in his meticulously crafted dishes.

This is his tenth book in the On a Plate series. Previous editions have included Glasgow, Edinburgh, Scotland, Manchester, Dublin and London.